The Cyber Blueprint

Quickly Learn How to Become a Cyber-security Specialist, Develop the Skills Needed for Immediate Employment, and Create a Road Map for a Lucrative Career

André Edmond

PUBLISHED BY IME

Publishing Group DISCLAIMER AND/OR LEGAL NOTICES

While all attempts have been made to verify the information provided in this book and its ancillary materials, neither the author or the publisher assume any responsibility for errors, inaccuracies or omissions and is not responsible for any financial loss by consumer in any manner. Any slights of people or organizations are unintentional. If advice concerning legal, financial, accounting, or related matters is needed, the service of a qualified professional should be sought. This book and its associated axillary materials, including verbal and written training, is not intended for use as a source of legal, financial, or accounting advice. You should be aware of the various laws governing business transactions or other business practices in your particular geographical location.

EARNINGS AND INCOME DISCLAIMER

With respect to the reliability, accuracy, timeliness, usefulness, adequacy, completeness, and/or suitability of information provided in the book, Andre Edmond and IME Publishing Group its Partners Associates Affiliates Consultants and/or presenters make no warranties guarantees representations or claims of any kind. Readers' results will vary depending on a number of factors. Any and all claims or representations as to income earnings are not to be considered and average earnings. Testimonials are not representative. This book and all products and services are for educational and informational purposes only. Use caution and see the advice of qualified professionals. Check with your accountant, attorney, or professional adviser before acting on this or any information. You agreed that Andre Edmond and IME Publishing Group is not responsible for the success or failure of your personal, business, health or financial decisions relating to any information presented by Andre Edmond and IME Publishing Group or Company products/ services. Earnings potential is entirely dependent on the efforts, skills, and application of the individual person. Exercises and ideas in the information materials offered are simply opinion or experience, and thus, should not be misinterpreted as promises, typical results or guarantees (expressed or implied). The author and the publisher Andre Edmond, IME Publishing Group (IME or any IME Representatives) Shall in no way, under any circumstances be held liable to any party (or third-party) for any direct, indirect, punitive, special, incidental or other consequential damages arising directly or indirectly from any use of books, materials and or seminar trainings, which is provided "as is," and without bwarranties Andre Edmond / IME Publishing Group.

Any examples, stories, references, or case studies are for illustrative purposes only and should not be interpreted as testimonies and/or examples of what readers and/ or consumers are generally expected from the

IME Publishing Group
1990 N California Blvd. Suite 20 PMB 1065
Walnut Creek, California 94596

1-866-726-6563
www.IMEPublishingGroup.com
Andre Edmond -1st ed.

This is a step-by-step guide to cybersecurity to help aspiring cybersecurity professionals get started.

https://www.mycyberblueprint.com/unlock-your-potentials-and-go-from-novice-to-cybersecurity-ninja-in-no-time

https://bit.ly/47FU3OE

Table of Contents

Forward

In an age where our lives are intricately woven into the fabric of the digital realm, the need for robust cybersecurity measures has never been more pressing. As we navigate the vast landscape of cyberspace, the ever-present risks and threats are a stark reminder of the importance of safeguarding our digital assets and infrastructure. *The Cyber Blueprint* is a definitive guide for those seeking to break into cybersecurity or enhance their cybersecurity skill set. The author, Andre Edmond, has leveraged his wealth of knowledge and years of experience safeguarding organizations' assets and mentoring young cybersecurity professionals to outlay a comprehensive yet clear roadmap for individuals aspiring to become cybersecurity specialists, providing them with the knowledge and skills necessary to thrive in this dynamic field.

The journey begins with an exploration of the foundational concepts in cybersecurity. From the historical origins of information security to its evolution into the modern-day cybersecurity landscape, readers are equipped with a solid understanding of the principles that underpin this critical field. As we delve deeper, the book highlights the paramount importance of cybersecurity in the digital age. As we continue to embrace innovative and disruptive technology in a digitalized world, protecting data, financial systems, national security, and critical infrastructure hinges upon the vigilance and expertise of cybersecurity professionals currently in short supply. Thus, this book could not have come at a much better time as organizations struggle to optimize their cybersecurity resources globally.

Understanding cyber threats and vulnerabilities is essential for any aspiring cybersecurity professional. By meticulously examining threat actors, attack vectors, and security breaches, readers gain insight into the ever-evolving landscape of cyber warfare. The information presented will give the readers insight into strategies for maintaining defensible digital assets. Central to the discussion is the CIA Triad— confidentiality, integrity, and availability—which forms the cornerstone of any effective cybersecurity program. This book clearly lays out these concepts as the building blocks of any organizational cybersecurity program in an easily digestible manner. By emphasizing these fundamental principles, the author furnishes the readers with the framework necessary to design robust security measures.

The Cyber Blueprint sheds light on the distinction between data security and data privacy, exploring the legal and regulatory frameworks that govern the protection of sensitive information. From GDPR to HIPAA, readers gain an understanding of the compliance standards that shape cybersecurity practices. The book thus emphasizes security requirements and provides insights into compliance considerations for an all-around appreciation of factors that drive cybersecurity programs in organizations. Perhaps most importantly, the book introduces the concept of security and privacy by design, advocating for a proactive approach to embedding security considerations into the fabric of our digital systems and products. By championing this approach, readers are empowered to mitigate risks and enhance resilience in an increasingly interconnected world.

In closing, *The Cyber Blueprint* is a beacon of knowledge and guidance for those who dare to venture into cybersecurity. The book also provides valuable resources and references as essential guides to a career in cybersecurity. With its comprehensive insights and practical guidance, this book is not just a roadmap for a lucrative cybersecurity career but a manifesto for safeguarding the digital future.

Dr. Abraham O. Okomanyi, DBA, PMP, TOGAF®9, CISSP®, CCSP®

Chapter 1:
Intro to Cybersecurity

This book will delve into the complex and critical world of cybersecurity. Our journey will begin by defining cybersecurity and exploring its objectives. We will then take a historical look back to the 1970s, when Bob Thomas created the first computer virus marking the inception of cybersecurity as we know it today.

In the first four chapters, we will cover the following topics:

1. **The Importance of Digital Transformation:** We will discuss how digital transformation is vital for business survival, exploring its positive and negative aspects. We will examine the impact of data breaches on companies and consumers, highlighting why cybersecurity is crucial for financial, national, and infrastructure security.

2. **Identifying Threat Actors and Attack Vectors:** We will explore the various threat actors and the attack pathways they use to breach companies. This will include discussions on malware attacks, phishing attacks, social engineering attacks, distributed denial of service attacks, and zero-day exploits. We will outline strategies companies can employ to reduce the risk of being breached.

3. **Understanding the CIA Triad:** We will delve into the principles of confidentiality, integrity, and availability (CIA Triad) and discuss how they form the foundation of cybersecurity. We will examine different attacks that target each aspect of the triad and explore mitigation techniques.

4. **Balancing Security and Privacy:** Lastly, we will explore the intricate relationship between security and privacy. We will discuss government regulations such as GDPR, CCPA, and HIPAA, which aim to protect individual privacy rights. We will delve into the concept of security and privacy by design, outlining its seven principles and how they can be implemented effectively.

By the end of these chapters, you will have gained a solid understanding of cybersecurity fundamentals, setting the stage for deeper exploration into more advanced topics in subsequent chapters. Before going any further, let's start by explaining information security and cybersecurity.

What is Information Security?

Contrary to widespread assumptions, protecting sensitive information against disclosure is not a new invention. According to historical records, the ancient Greeks employed a device called the Scytale to encrypt messages. Another famous example is the Caesar Cipher, named after Julius Caesar, the Roman Emperor, which uses a simple substitution cipher to protect military communications. Fast forward to February 1883, when Auguste Kerckhoffs, a Dutch linguist and professor of German, published an article in the *Journal of Military Science* that provided one of the basic foundations of modern cryptography. It is called Kerckhoffs' Principle. Then, in the 20th century, the Germans heavily used the Enigma machine for communication during World War II. For centuries, armies have used encryption to secure information and communication.

Information security is a broad term encompassing the protection of all forms of information, whether in physical or digital form. It includes strategies, policies, and measures to ensure information confidentiality, integrity, and availability, the three principles of the CIA Triad that we will examine later in the book.

The goal of information security is to protect data, the most valuable asset of a company, against unauthorized access, modification, removal, and deletion. This ensures confidentiality, integrity, and availability of the data. That is the reason information security is also referred to as data security. The data can be at rest or in storage, meaning it is not being used or accessed. It can be in transit, being transmitted over the network or the Internet. Finally, the data may be in use, which denotes that a system or an individual be accessing or using it. We usually use the word data when we are talking about information. However, they are not the same. Data is raw facts or statistics like a date of birth, weight, or temperature. But when you combine, for example, a date of birth with the full name and weight of an individual, you have information, which is the organization or interpretation of the data. Information security is aimed at protecting three types of data, as stated below.

The first type of data is called Personally Identifiable Information (PII), a term used to describe sensitive information such as a full name, Social Security number, or driver's license information that can identify a person. The second one is Protected Health Information (PHI). This includes individuals' medical information. Third is sensitive and classified information. This includes trade secrets, intellectual property, military, and national security information. Every security program relies on confidentiality, integrity, and availability. These three principles are commonly referred to as the CIA Triad, which we will cover in more detail later in the book.

Cybersecurity

Let's discuss cybersecurity. It's a branch of information security dedicated to safeguarding computers, networks, and digital assets in cyberspace from unauthorized access, alteration, or disruption. In the cyber-realm, assets refer to anything valuable to an organization, such as data, servers, or personnel. Assets are categorized into two types:

critical and non-critical. Critical assets are essential for the company's operations and revenue generation, while non-critical assets wouldn't impact the company's functioning or earnings if they were unavailable.

Cybersecurity relies on the CIA Triad to protect a company against cyber threats. The need for cybersecurity started in the 1970s when Bob Thomas, an ARPANET developer, created the first computer worm called the Creeper. The ARPANET, which stands for Advanced Research Projects Agency Network, was the first network created before the Internet. Bob Thomas's program could move from one machine to another by itself.

Shortly after that, Ray Tomlinson, the creator of the first email program for the ARPANET, created an enhanced version of the program that replicated itself. Later, he wrote the Reaper program, which moved through the ARPANET to remove the Creeper.

With the creation of the Internet and computers, came new challenges for information security. The focus shifted to securing computer systems, networks, and data. Concepts like firewalls, antivirus software, and secure protocols became essential. It is important to know that even though cybersecurity's goal is to protect a company from cyber threats, there isn't 100% security. There will always be opportunities for data breaches. It is impossible for an operable company to have 100% security. For a company to have 1 00% security, it would have to shut down its computers and network and put everything behind a secure door, rendering the company inoperable. As you know, for a company to exist and make money, it must take risks. Cybersecurity is about understanding and managing these risks.

The Importance of Cybersecurity in the Digital Age

In this section, we will explore the critical importance of cybersecurity in today's digital landscape. We will investigate the phenomenon of digital transformation and its profound impact on reshaping how we conduct business and interact with technology. However, alongside these advancements come inherent risks and vulnerabilities that must be addressed.

From the pervasive threat of cyberattacks to the potential consequences of data breaches, identity theft, and ransomware incidents, the dangers posed by cyber threats are ever-present in our interconnected world. Without adequate cybersecurity measures in place, individuals, businesses, and even entire nations are susceptible to substantial harm and exploitation. Understanding the importance of cybersecurity empowers you to proactively protect yourself and your digital assets from potential threats and breaches.

Digital Transformation

Digital transformation uses technology to transform how a business operates to create new products or services for customer needs. Due to digital transformation, the way we shop, entertain ourselves, and conduct business has undergone significant changes. For instance, we can now deposit a check into our bank account using our mobile phone. The pandemic further accelerated this shift, transitioning many in-person jobs to remote work settings, all made possible by advancements in digital technology.

Digital transformation can even be a matter of survival for a company. An example is what happened with the video rental company Blockbuster and its competitor, Netflix. Blockbuster was a well-known video rental company that started in the mid-1980s and dominated the movie rental business until the mid-2000s. While the world was increasingly moving to the Internet to conduct business, its management did not change how it operated.

They kept the same business model, relying on brick-and-mortar stores to conduct business. They had over 60,000 stores worldwide, while Netflix, which started as a company that rented DVDs by mail in the mid-1990s, quickly adapted, and transformed itself into a streaming service, now making over $8 billion a year, while Blockbuster went out of business. As you can see from this example, digital transformation is necessary for a company to survive in this digital age.

However, digital transformation also has disadvantages, such as an increased risk of cyber-attacks and data breaches. Companies are using the cloud to stay competitive and are putting more and more data in the cloud. Because of a lack of expertise or due diligence, cloud environments are often misconfigured. Vulnerabilities are not promptly remediated, making it easy for threat actors to access the data. Data has become a valuable asset, and companies use it to create new products and services and for marketing. Threat actors are also after the same data because of the financial incentive, so a robust cybersecurity program is vital to protecting the organization's network and data.

The Impact of Data Breaches

A data breach is when a threat actor can access a company's data without their consent, and depending on their intent, they can steal the data by making a copy, deleting it, or changing it. Data breaches and cyberattacks have become so routine and widespread that it feels weird not to hear about them in the news.

People sometimes use the term data leak when discussing a data breach. However, the two terms are different. A data breach is an intentional attack, while a data leak is when a company's data is exposed accidentally on the Internet, either by employees posting something they weren't supposed to, emailing an unencrypted file that contains sensitive information, or a misconfigured Amazon S3 bucket. It can also happen through a loss of mobile devices or storage media.

According to an article on itgovernance.co.uk, June 2023 was a top month for cyberattacks, with the three most significant security incidents accounting for over 13 million breached records. Hackers were able to breach state governments, universities, the Department of Motor Vehicles in several states, financial institutions, and other small companies. Crypto-currency has made it easier for hackers to cash in on data breaches and ransomware attacks, as it is hard or even impossible to track a crypto transaction to a specific person. According to Techopedia, over 493 million attacks were detected by organizations in 2022.

A report from the Federal Trade Commission stated that in 2022, over 440,000 people were victims of credit fraud, and 156,000 were victims of bank fraud. If you have been a victim or know someone who has been, you see how this type of fraud can jeopardize your finances, put you under a lot of stress, and waste your time while clearing your credit and trying to recover your money.

The consequences of a data breach can be severe for the organization and its customers. The organization may face penalties from regulatory bodies, customer lawsuits, legal fees, breach remediation costs, damage to their reputation, loss of customers, and a decline in their stock value, contingent on the data that is accessed or pilfered by the threat actor. For individuals or customers, the bad actor can use their personal information for identity theft or worse. They can drain their bank account and stalk them on the Internet, which can cause a great deal of emotional distress.

Financial Security

Financial security is the ability to protect one's financial assets from cyberattacks. For example, a hacker can quickly gain unauthorized access to a person's online banking account and steal their money. That is why they use different methods to get users' credentials. Cybercriminals often use phishing emails, text messages, or websites to trick individuals into revealing sensitive information about their login credentials, credit card numbers, or banking details. Also, they use malicious software or malware to infect computers and mobile devices to steal credentials. As the convenience of online banking, shopping, and payment methods increases, so does the importance of cybersecurity awareness. Proactive measures, such as using secure passwords and enabling two-factor authentication wherever possible, will protect your account. You should also stay informed about emerging threats, adopt security practices, and leverage security features to protect your financial transactions in the digital landscape.

National Security

Cybersecurity is crucial for safeguarding national security interests. For example, governments have classified military and personal information about their citizens. Therefore, cyberattacks or data breaches can compromise sensitive data, which can cause communication disruption and cause critical defense systems to be infiltrated by the adversary.

They can also lead to cyber espionage, identity theft, and blackmail. Therefore, robust cybersecurity measures are essential to protect sensitive data and maintain national security.

Protecting Critical Infrastructure

Cybersecurity is vital in protecting critical infrastructure. For instance, in February 2021, an unknown hacker gained remote access to a Florida water supply and began dumping sodium hydroxide, a dangerous substance, into the water system. A few months later, in May 2021, a ransomware attack on the Colonial Pipeline by the Dark Side group, which is no longer in business, shut down its operations for almost five days. This causes long lines and high gas prices for millions across the southeastern United States. Colonial Pipeline had to pay the Dark Side group $4.4 million in cryptocurrency to restore its operating systems.

Because of the interconnected world we are living in, cyberattacks on critical infrastructure have been used as war tactics to shut down the activity and economy of a nation. A cyberattack in this sector can lead to significant economic losses, disrupt the supply chain, and undermine the stability of a nation. That is why cybersecurity is so vital to safeguarding critical infrastructure.

Privacy Concerns

Privacy is essential for all of us. It is unnecessary to do business with a company for them to acquire a lot of information about you. They can purchase the information from other companies called data brokers. When a malicious actor breaches a company, your personal information can be available to every-one on the web.

For example, if a bad actor breaches a healthcare provider, your health record is accessible to everyone. Anyone can access your complete medical records. Cybersecurity helps an organization comply with privacy regulations by protecting the data they have about you and limiting the amount of information they collect.

Tips

Here are two tips you can implement immediately to help protect your data and develop a security mindset.

1. Check to see if your password has been leaked on the Internet by going to this website: https://haveibeenpwned.com.

2. Be cautious about the information you share on social media and other online platforms. Avoid sharing sensitive personal or financial information that threat actors could use for malicious purposes.

Recap

This chapter has explored the concepts of information security and cybersecurity, highlighting their distinctions. We have traced the origins of information protection back to ancient civilizations, such as the Greeks and Romans, who utilized encryption techniques to secure their communications. We have delved into the significance of digital transformation in today's business landscape, emphasizing its role in revolutionizing various aspects of commerce, entertainment, and work. We also recognize the heightened risks of cyberattacks and data breaches accompanying increased digital exposure. We have examined the profound impacts of data breaches on companies and consumers, underscoring the importance of cybersecurity for safeguarding financial, national, and infrastructure security.

In Chapter 2, we will discuss cybersecurity threats and the people behind them, as well as their objectives. We'll also share strategies companies can use to protect themselves.

The glossary has common terms used in IT and cybersecurity that aspiring cybersecurity professionals need to know.

https://www.mycyberblueprint.com/the-cybersecurity-glossary

https://bit.ly/3Of6s5n

Chapter 2: Identifying Threat Actors and Attack Vectors

In this chapter, we will explore cyber threats, vulnerabilities, and security strategies. We will define security threats, identify threat actors and their motivations, and discuss zero-day vulnerabilities and exploits. We will examine the CIA Triad principles, cover security strategies for mitigating risks, and conclude by exploring Privacy by Design principles.

Cybersecurity Threats

A cybersecurity threat is a deliberate activity or action that can negatively impact an organization. It can result in data theft, data leakage, and the threat actor gaining access to a computer system or network. Some common categories of cyber threats are malware, ransomware, phishing, and distributed denial of service attacks.

Malware

Malware is malicious software designed by a threat actor intending to steal data and damage computer systems. Ransomware is also a type of malicious malware designed to prevent the company or end users from using their computers to access their data until they have paid a ransom.

Phishing Attacks

A phishing attack is a subtype of social engineering attack where cybercriminals impersonate a trusted contact and send fake emails to their victims to get them to reveal personal and sensitive information or to click on a malicious link that will install malware on their computers.

Distributed Denial of Service Attacks

A distributed denial of service attack occurs when cybercriminals send a lot of traffic or connection requests to a server or a website from multiple sources, causing the server to run out of resources. Therefore, legitimate users cannot access that server or website. An analogy would be when we used to have one phone line. While we used that phone line, anybody else who tried to call us could not reach us. All they got was a busy tone.

Threat Actors

A threat actor can be a single person, group, organization, or even a country involved in a targeted cyberattack. There are several types of threat actors, and they are grouped based on their objectives and motivations.

Career Criminals

This is the most common type of threat actor. They can be a group or a single individual, and their goal is financial gain. They will steal financial data like credit cards, bank information, HR data, and customer data, which they will resell on the dark web or use for identity theft. As part of their arsenal, they will use phishing attacks, ransomware, malware, social engineering attacks, and other techniques to compromise their target.

State-Sponsored

Some state-sponsored actors engage in cyber espionage, sabotage, and cyber warfare to further their nation's interests. These actors also seek to destabilize countries, as evidenced by the 2013 incident where a group of Syrian hackers compromised The Associated Press Twitter account and falsely reported explosions at the White House, along with President Obama being injured. This fake news caused the Dow Jones to plummet by 150 points, resulting in a loss of $136 billion in equity market value. State-sponsored actors are often driven by nationalism and typically possess advanced capabilities and substantial resources to achieve their objectives.

Hacktivists

Hacktivists are driven by political, social, or ideological causes, aiming to expose what they perceive as an organization's wrongdoing and raise awareness about specific issues. They may assist citizens in bypassing government censorship to access restricted websites or social media platforms for human rights advocacy. Some well-known activist groups are Anonymous, Legion of Doom, and Chaos Computer Club.

Script Kiddies

The script kiddies group consists of inexperienced individuals exploring hacking, often using pre-existing tools and techniques to carry out attacks either for amusement or to gain recognition from others.

Insider Threat Actors

It is a security risk posed by employees, contractors, or business partners who have access to an organization's networks, systems, or data. These individuals may intentionally or unintentionally misuse their access privileges to harm the organization by stealing sensitive information, committing fraud, sabotaging operations, or compromising security through actions like falling victim to phishing attacks or downloading malware. Such insider threats can jeopardize an organization's data security, integrity, and overall business functionality.

Corporate Espionage

Corporate competitors or other entities may use cyber espionage to gather sensitive information, trade secrets, and intellectual property to gain a competitive edge or damage a competitor's brand.

Barring inexperienced groups such as the Script Kiddies, the other threat actors usually have many skills, tools, resources, and techniques to carry out their malicious activities. The path or means the threat actors use to deliver their payload or to compromise a company is called an attack vector. Let's talk about a few of them.

Attack Vectors

Social Engineering

Social engineering is an extremely effective attack vector employed by threat actors. Cybercriminals employ these strategies to trick victims into disclosing personal information about them or the company they work for, information that will enable them to gain access to the organization. For instance, they may pose as help desk personnel or representatives from other departments, contacting victims via phone to elicit sensitive details or prompt them to take certain actions. Alternatively, they may send deceptive emails purporting to be from trusted sources, containing malicious attachments or links.

Upon clicking these links or opening attachments, victims unwittingly download malware or inadvertently surrender their credentials. Other social engineering techniques are business email compromise, spear phishing, whaling, smishing, and tailgating.

Software Vulnerability

Another attack vector is finding and exploiting software vulnerability. A vulnerability is a security flaw or weakness in the software code, and the attacker can use that vulnerability to access the company's network.

Password Attacks

A password attack is a way malicious actors can access an account using techniques such as brute-forcing, credential stuffing, and password spraying. A brute-forcing attack is a trial-and-error method attackers use to get someone's login credentials. It can be manual, but often they use automated tools to speed up the process.

Credential Stuffing: This method involves the attackers using previously exposed login credentials from past data breaches. They will use these credentials to log into a user's other accounts. The success rate can be great, as the attackers know most people usually reuse their passwords or credentials on several websites.

Password Spraying: here attackers attempt to authenticate by using the same password across multiple accounts within the same application. Most people like to use simple and predictable passwords. So, the threat actors will try one password against many accounts before moving on to another password or account. This technique prevents account lockout, which usually happens when using a brute-force attack.

Supply Chain Attack

A supply chain attack happens when threat actors infiltrate a company's internal network or computer systems by using one of their vendors. The compromised vendor is usually a trusted partner that provides a service or a product. To illustrate, the bad actor knows there's a particular piece of software that several companies use in the financial industry. What they will do is compromise the software vendor and then insert malicious code or a backdoor into the software source code.

This way, they can access the network of all companies in the financial industry using that software. A recent example of a supply chain attack occurred with SolarWinds. Attackers were able to implant a backdoor into popular networking software used by government agencies and enterprises. The backdoor allowed the bad actors to access thousands of corporate and government servers. Ultimately, at least 250 organizations were breached because of this supply chain attack. Threat actors can also compromise hardware manufacturers by planting their malicious code into the device firmware. This will allow access to the network or computer systems of the buyers.

Island Hopping or Leap Frogging: This attack is very targeted. The malicious actors usually go after large corporations such as Microsoft or Amazon. They will take the time to research what smaller vendors those big corporations are using and then compromise one or several small companies until they reach the target. They know those smaller companies usually have less security.

Zero-Day Vulnerabilities

A zero-day vulnerability is a broad term used to describe a recently discovered vulnerability that hackers can use or have been using to attack a system. It also means that the vendor or the developer had zero time to fix the security flaw before it was exploited by hackers.

These hackers encompass a variety of individuals and groups, including cybercriminals, activists, hacktivists, and state-sponsored actors. With state-sponsored actors, their attacks are often referred to as Advanced Persistent Threats (APTs). An APT comprises ongoing, covert attacks orchestrated by individuals, groups, or nation-states targeting specific entities such as nations or large corporations, sometimes both. These attacks are typically politically motivated, though financial gain may also be a factor. The term "advanced" highlights these actors' sophisticated techniques and capabilities, including their adeptness at exploiting zero-day vulnerabilities. They exhibit persistence by continually monitoring and attacking their targets over extended periods of time to gather intelligence or steal sensitive information.

Two other zero-day terms are often used: zero-day exploit and zero-day attack. A zero-day exploit is the method or means the attackers use to exploit the system with a previously unknown vulnerability. As explained earlier, an attack is the use of a zero-day exploit to cause damage or take over a system.

Security Strategies to Reduce Risks

Organizations need security strategies to proactively fight and prevent cyber threats. Here is a short list of strategies that can be implemented.

1. **Perform a risk assessment:** A company needs to identify potential vulnerabilities and risks to its assets, processes, and infrastructure that can negatively affect them and have controls in place to manage these risks.

2. **Provide compliance and security awareness training to employees:** The training will help them identify social engineering and phishing attacks. This will prevent them from clicking on a link or opening an attachment that might have malware.

3. **Create security policies and procedures:** It is a must for a company to develop, implement, and enforce security policies and procedures for its employees to follow.

4. **Strict access control:** Implementing strict access controls such as the least privileged principle and multifactor authentication (MFA) for strong authentication will help a company defend against password attacks.

5. **Vulnerability management:** Vulnerability management is an ongoing, proactive process designed to safeguard your computer systems, networks, and business applications against cyberattacks and data breaches. As you know, threat actors like to exploit vulnerabilities. So having a solid vulnerability management process to keep the software, operating systems, and applications up to date is necessary.

6. **Use firewalls, intrusion detection systems, and intrusion prevention systems:** A company must have firewalls, IDS, and IPS to monitor and block suspicious activities.

7. **Data encryption:** Encrypting sensitive data makes it more difficult for threat actors to access and renders it unusable to them without the decryption key.

8. **Security Information and Event Management (SIEM):** Use a SIEM to monitor activity and access across the network and to quickly identify, investigate, and respond to security threats.

9. **Business continuity and disaster recovery:** Having a business continuity and disaster recovery plan will help to protect the organization, systems, data, services, and customers from cyberattacks. That also includes regular backups and testing to ensure they can be successfully restored in case of an attack. A robust business continuity and disaster recovery (BCDR) plan is essential for organizations to protect their systems, data, services, and customers from cyberattacks by minimizing downtime and

preserving data integrity through backup and recovery procedures. This proactive approach enhances cyber resilience, enabling organizations to identify and mitigate potential threats effectively. Implementing a BCDR plan fosters customer trust by demonstrating preparedness and compliance with regulatory requirements, while also facilitating clear communication and coordination during cyber incidents. Overall, a well-developed BCDR plan is crucial for maintaining business continuity, reducing the impact of cyberattacks, and safeguarding the organization's reputation in today's interconnected cyber landscape.

10. **Third-party risk management:** Third-party risk manage-ment plays a crucial role in continuously monitoring a vendor's security posture by establishing clear criteria and standards that vendors must adhere to regarding cybersecurity practices and protocols. A regular risk assessment and audit can help organizations identify potential vulnerabilities and weaknesses in their vendors' security measures. This proactive approach enables organizations to collaborate with vendors to address and mitigate security risks promptly, ensuring that vendors maintain a robust and resilient security posture aligned with industry best practices and regulatory requirements.

11. **Have a robust incident response plan:** A comprehensive incident response plan should outline steps to take in case of a security incident or breach, such as how to detect, contain, eradicate, and recover from an incident. This will help a company quickly address and respond to an incident.

Tips

Tips to help protect yourself against cyber threats.

1. You should be careful when you receive an email with an attachment or a link, especially if it is from someone you don't know or you did not expect to receive such an email. As you

recall, malicious actors use this threat vector to infect your computer and steal your personal information. Even if you receive an email from somebody that you know, if it is suspicious, pick up the phone and ask them if they intended to send you this email, as their email or even their computer may have been compromised.

2. Use a different password for each account to protect yourself against a password attack. If a company offers two-factor authentication (2FA), make sure you use it to protect your accounts.

3. Share your knowledge about cybersecurity best practices with friends, family, and colleagues. Encourage them to follow these tips and stay vigilant against cyber threats.

Recap

We have identified various threat actors and their objectives, elucidating the diverse attack vectors they employ, including malware, phishing, social engineering, distributed denial of service attacks, and zero-day exploits. We have also discussed strategies for mitigating these risks.

In Chapter 3, we'll cover a fundamental concept in cybersecurity—the Confidentiality, Integrity, and Availability (CIA) Triad. Understanding these principles is essential for designing secure systems and protecting sensitive data.

Chapter 3: Confidentiality, Integrity, and Availability (CIA) Triad

This chapter explores the fundamental principles of security, namely confidentiality, integrity, and availability, collectively known as the CIA Triad or Iron Triad. We'll investigate the significance of these principles as the cornerstone of any cybersecurity program. We will examine various attacks targeting these principles and strategies to mitigate them. We'll examine how the CIA Triad should ideally function synergistically, as well as the challenges organizations face in achieving this synergy. We'll explore the diverse cybersecurity priorities that organizations may prioritize.

Confidentiality

Confidentiality is the first principle. Confidentiality is about protecting data from unauthorized access, use, or disclosure. When we are talking about unauthorized access, it means not only from hackers but also from personnel that are not supposed to have access to the data. For example, an administrator who is not part of the payroll department should not have access to payroll data. To ensure confidentiality, the company needs to know where its data is and in what state it is.

Confidentiality applies to all three states. Data can be in transit or on the wire, like when exchanging information with someone via email. It can be at rest or in storage, like in a database or on a flash drive. It can be in use, like when you are running a query on a payroll database or using a spreadsheet of employees' payroll information.

Attacks On Confidentiality

Interception attack: An interception attack is when a threat actor intercepts the data in transit by placing themselves in the middle of the communication. You can also use a sniffer to read the transmitted information if the data is not encrypted.

Shoulder Surfing: For instance, the malicious actor can stand over the shoulder of another employee to read sensitive information while entering their password or accessing confidential information. We also have password attacks that were covered earlier, where the threat actors gain access to the computer systems to access the data. Phishing and social engineering attacks are another type of attack used to breach the confidentiality of a system.

Unintentional Violations: Often, unauthorized disclosure results from human errors, oversight, and a lack of skills. Something that happens frequently is when an employee sends a fax or an email containing sensitive information to the wrong party, or a payroll employee prints a file but leaves it unattended on the printer, and someone else picks it up.

System Misconfiguration: can have a system miscon-figuration, which grants access to sensitive data to the wrong person.

Countermeasures To Protect Confidentiality

When talking about a countermeasure, we are also referring to security controls that a company can put in place to prevent something from happening or to protect the data or the system.

Encryption: The number one countermeasure is encryption. Encrypting the hard drive with BitLocker or the database with symmetric encryption can protect the data at rest. For data on the wire, the file can be encrypted before being transmitted, like encrypting an attachment before emailing or using an encrypted channel like TLS when sending information over the wire. An example is when you are accessing your bank account online. If you look in the upper left corner of the URL, the padlock icon is an indication that transferring the data over the wire is encrypted.

Secure Printing: Use secure print functionality when printing confidential documents. When you send a print request to the printer, it is queued until you go to the printer and badge in to release the job.

Screen Filter: With shoulder surfing, using a screen filter can prevent somebody standing over your shoulder from being able to read the information.

Security Awareness Training: Security awareness training educates individuals about safeguarding confidential information and the potential risks associated with unauthorized access or disclosure. By increasing awareness and understanding of security policies, procedures, and best practices, employees are better equipped to identify and mitigate potential threats, enhancing the protection of confidentiality within an organization.

Data Classification: Data classification involves classifying data based on its sensitivity, importance, and regulatory requirements to ensure appropriate handling, storage, and protection measures are applied. By systematically classifying data into categories such as public, internal, confidential, or restricted, organizations can implement tailored security controls, access permissions, and encryption. This structured approach enables organizations to prioritize protection efforts, allocate resources effectively, and safeguard sensitive information from unauthorized access, enhancing the protection of confidentiality and overall data security.

Least Privilege Principle: The principle of least privilege restricts the access rights granted to users, ensuring individuals only have the permissions necessary for their specific tasks. Providing limited access to essential functions and data can reduce the risk of unauthorized access, data breaches, and inadvertent disclosure of sensitive data, strengthening confidentiality and reducing potential security vulnerabilities.

Integrity

Integrity is about ensuring that the data remains accurate and unaltered for its entire life cycle. When the data is in transit, at rest, or in use, it needs to be protected from unauthorized modification by both authorized and unauthorized users. Even though someone is authorized to access the data, they should not be able to change it without the consent and knowledge of the owner. Measures should be put in place to preserve the integrity of the data.

Besides the data, we also need to preserve the integrity of the operating system and programs by manipulating the data. If the system where the data is located is compromised, the data will be compromised as well.

Attacks on Integrity

Salami Attack: A salami attack is when a malicious actor makes a series of minor changes to the data, resulting in a more significant attack when combined.

To illustrate, a malicious actor working at a bank withdraws a penny from thousands of accounts each month, which is a small amount, but combined, it is a considerable sum.

System Modification: Unauthorized modifications to the system, whether caused by human errors or malware attacks, can cause data corruption, alteration, or deletion, leading to inaccurate information being processed or retrieved. This can have severe consequences, such as incorrect decision-making, financial losses, damaged reputations, or regulatory non-compliance.

Man-In-The-Middle (MitM): Data in transit is susceptible to man-in-the-middle attack or interception attack. A man-in-the-middle attack occurs when a malicious actor intercepts. For instance, during an online transaction, an attacker could intercept and modify the payment details or transaction amount, leading to financial fraud or unauthorized fund transfers. Similarly, in a communication involving sensitive information like passwords, personal data, or confidential documents, the attacker could alter the content, leading to misinformation, identity theft, or unauthorized access to sensitive data.

Unintentional Mistakes: Human errors can also pose secur-ity risks, like a database administrator accidentally deleting a table from the customer database. An employee updating an application on the production server without obtaining approval from the Change Advisory Board can unintentionally alter the data.

Countermeasures To Protect Integrity

Data confidentiality goes hand in hand with integrity. Without confidentiality, we can't be sure the data wasn't modified.

Access Control: Limiting access to sensitive data and systems to authorized individuals or roles through strong authentication and authorization mechanisms.

Monitoring and Auditing: Regularly monitoring and auditing system activities, user actions, and data access to detect and investigate unauthorized or suspicious activities promptly. File integrity monitoring can also monitor changes to the data.

Implementing Data Validation: Data validation checks whether the input, output, and transactions are valid to ensure that only valid and authorized data are processed and stored. For example, a user filling out a form mistakenly enters a phone number instead of their Social Security number. The application will reject it because of a mismatch in the expected character, type, format, or range. Other measures that will protect the integrity of systems are intrusion detection systems and intrusion protection systems.

Hashing Algorithms or Checksums: Hashing and checksums are cryptographic techniques to verify data integrity and detect unauthorized modifications or tampering. They can indicate whether data has been altered while at rest, in transit, or in use. However, they won't tell us who made the change or whether an authorized user made it.

Availability

Availability ensures that the information, data, network, or system is available to authorized users when needed. For that, we need to eliminate a Single Point Of Failure (SPOF). There are numerous threats to availability.

Threats on Availability

Distributed Denial of Service (DDoS) Attacks: In a DDoS attack, multiple compromised systems (botnets) flood a targeted system, network, or service with a massive traffic volume, overwhelming its resources and causing it to become slow or unresponsive. For example, a DDoS attack may target an e-commerce website during a major sale event, preventing customers from accessing the site and making purchases.

Insider Threat: An employee intentionally deletes critical data or misconfigures network settings, leading to service outages or system failures.

Physical Attacks: Physical attacks involve physically damaging or destroying an organization's hardware, infrastructure, or facilities.

Environmental Threats: Similarly, a power outage at a data center can disrupt the normal operation of an organization's information systems, networks, and services, leading to downtime and service interruptions. There are also natural disasters like heat waves, floods, hurricanes, and tornadoes. All these events can prevent authorized users from accessing the system or data when needed.

Countermeasures To Protect Availability

DDoS Mitigation Controls: Mitigating DDoS attacks involves deploying dedicated protection solutions, increasing network bandwidth, and configuring firewall rules to filter and block malicious traffic, safeguarding systems and services from disruptions. Utilizing Content Delivery Network (CDN) services and implementing continuous network monitoring and anomaly detection can help identify and mitigate DDoS attack patterns, minimizing downtime and service degradation. Using DDoS mitigation service companies like CloudFlare, which offer DDoS protection services, we will discuss more about these controls later on in this book.

Access Control: To mitigate the insider threat risks, we must implement access controls, least privilege principles, and strong authentication to limit and monitor user access to sensitive systems and data.

Redundant Systems and Failover Clusters: Deploying redundant hardware, systems, and failover clusters to automatically redirect traffic, workload, or services to alternate resources or locations in the event of a system failure or service disruption.

Availability also relies on the first two principles, confidentiality and integrity. Without confidentiality and integrity, we cannot have availability. So these three principles all work together, and that's why reason they are called the building blocks of the information security program.

CIA Triad in Action

For a company to establish a strong cybersecurity program, these three principles—confidentiality, integrity, and availability—must harmoniously coexist. However, priorities can vary. For instance, governments handling national security information or companies like Apple may prioritize keeping intellectual property confidential above ensuring integrity and availability. On the other hand, airline companies will prioritize integrity and availability since they must provide accurate and up-to-date information so passengers don't miss their flights. That said, let's consider other challenges of the CIA Triad.

CIA Triad Challenges

Now, let's examine some challenges a company may encounter in balancing the three principles.

Confidentiality vs Availability

The first one is between confidentiality and availability. As we have discussed earlier, confidentiality is about limiting access to the data to authorized users only. One control that a company can implement to maintain confidentiality is strict access control. By doing so, the data that used to be readily available to users is no longer accessible because they need to be authorized first to gain access to the data.

Confidentiality vs Integrity

Don't forget that integrity is about ensuring the data is free from unintended modifications or distortions. One control we can implement is logging and monitoring to catch alterations to the data. While this measure will help with integrity, it may inadvertently expose sensitive data or information to unauthorized users. To illustrate, if a financial institution monitors activities on user's accounts and is not careful, it can expose customer account details in logs to a security analyst who is not supposed to have access to this type of data as part of their job.

Integrity vs Availability

An organization may prioritize uptime, meaning availability, over integrity through security patching or system maintenance. Therefore, the company will delay installing critical software patches to avoid temporary downtime.

Ways to Address These Challenges

To address these challenges, a company can implement some of these strategies outlined below.

1. **Layered Security Approach:** A layered security approach is a form of redundancy that can protect a company against a single point of failure. As an illustration, they need to have two servers that are working in parallel instead of one. So when they need to patch one system, the other one will be available.

2. **Performing a Risk Assessment:** A risk assessment will allow a company to identify threats and vulnerabilities that can affect its posture. During the assessment, the company will prioritize its risks based on criticality and manage them accordingly.

3. **Data-Centric Approach:** Everything we do in security or cybersecurity is about protecting the data from unauthorized access. The bad actors are after the data because it is valuable, so using a data-centric approach, an organization will establish security to protect the data. To protect and secure the company's critical information, it is essential first to identify and know what system it is stored on. With this knowledge, appropriate security measures can be implemented accordingly.

Tips

Tips to protect you against fake news and malicious websites.

1. To avoid spreading misinformation or falling victim to disinformation campaigns, you should critically evaluate and verify information you found online for authenticity by checking the website or blogs reputation, the author and also cross check the information with multiple sources.

2. Look at the website's domain and URL to see if they match the reputable organization or entity they claim to represent. Be wary of websites with unusual or misspelled domain names, as they could imitate legitimate sites to deceive visitors.

Recap

We have explored the fundamental principles of the CIA Triad or Iron Triangle, namely confidentiality, integrity, and availability, outlining different attacks on these principles and countermeasures to mitigate them. Lastly, we discussed how companies may face in balancing these principles and strategies they can follow to overcome them.

In Chapter 4, we are going to talk about data security and privacy. Their importance in protecting our personal information. We'll also discuss data privacy regulations to protect individuals' personal information.

Chapter 4:
Data Security and Data Privacy

This chapter examines the differences between data security and data privacy, defining each concept and highlighting their interrelationship. We will explore the importance of companies balancing security and privacy and address legal and regulatory considerations to enhance privacy. We'll discuss security measures and processes like data minimization and anonymization that can bolster data privacy and security. We will introduce the principle of Privacy by Design and conclude by outlining the seven Privacy by Design Principles and how companies can implement them effectively.

Data Security vs Data Privacy

When you think of data privacy, what comes to mind? Perhaps Google, Facebook, or Equifax, given the vast amount of data they possess about us.

While this is true, there are also over 4,000 companies worldwide whose primary business is to collect and sell your personal data. This practice is known as data brokering. Why do we mention this? Because these companies cannot underestimate the importance of safeguarding your data from malicious actors and preventing its misuse. It is common to hear terms like data privacy and data security being misused in the news. What are data privacy and data security? While both concepts are crucial for protecting information, they have distinct focuses and considerations.

As we stated earlier, data security is about safeguarding the data against malicious threats and unauthorized access. To achieve data security, a company will use security controls such as access restriction, data encryption, data loss prevention tools, and technologies such as firewalls, intrusion detection systems, and tokenization, which we will explain shortly. Data security focuses on protecting the data from being breached or leaked, either by an unauthorized user or external threat actor.

Privacy is concerned with ensuring the data is processed, stored, and transmitted in compliance with applicable laws and regulations. It also means the company should inform individuals upfront of which data types or data elements they will collect, for what purposes, and with whom they will share the data. Once permission is received from consumers or end users, the company can start collecting the data and use it for the intended purposes.

So, what data elements are they collecting? They collect names, addresses, dates of birth, marital status, shopping habits, Internet surfing habits, and much more.

That's why we often encounter privacy notices or terms and conditions when visiting a website, even though they're intentionally lengthy to discourage us from reading them thoroughly. However, it's important to invest time in understanding what we're agreeing to or consenting to. Banks and healthcare providers also provide privacy notices. While securing data is crucial, as previously explained, maintaining privacy requires companies to use the collected data only for their intended purposes and adhere to relevant laws and regulations.

Interestingly, while we can have data security without data privacy, data privacy cannot exist without security. Understanding the distinction between security and privacy is crucial for businesses to develop comprehensive cybersecurity strategies. While focusing solely on security measures can protect data from breaches and unauthorized access, neglecting privacy can lead to legal and regulatory issues, damage to reputation, and loss of customer trust. Therefore, it's not ideal for a company to only prioritize security; they must also consider privacy to ensure they comply with regulations, maintain customer trust, and protect their brand reputation.

Balancing Security and Privacy

With the rise of cyberattacks and the fear of terrorist acts, there is a need to protect individuals and organizations. Lately, in the name of security, companies, and governments collect a ton of information about their citizens and consumers using tracking technology and video surveillance at airports, office buildings, or on the street. While these measures can help catch criminals, they also raise privacy concerns. When organizations or governments collect more information than is necessary for a specific security purpose, there is a risk that this data could be misused or accessed without proper authorization.

Balancing security and privacy can be very challenging, as security measures can sometimes infringe on privacy rights. Some people argue that privacy is a fundamental right that should be protected at all costs, while others say that security outweighs privacy rights. These two principles are both critical to our society. Privacy is vital for several reasons, including human dignity, preventing human rights abuses, and freedom of expression.

The Challenge

Another instance is the fight between the government and Apple to provide access to encrypted data on iPhones for national security. Apple argues that doing that will compromise privacy and security. This is where legal frameworks play a crucial role in establishing the boundaries between security measures and privacy rights, ensuring that individuals are protected from unwarranted intrusions into their private lives.

Legal and Regulatory Framework

Let's explore some data regulations that promote data security and privacy.

The General Data Protection Regulation (GDPR) is an international privacy and security law designed to protect EU citizens. It governs how companies can use, process, and store the personal data of EU citizens. Any entity that collects EU citizens' data is subject to this regulation. Also, a company that fails to follow GDPR requirements can be fined up to €10 million, or 2% of the worldwide annual revenue of the previous fiscal year. Facebook was fined €7 million and Google €10 million in 2022.

The California Consumer Privacy Act (CCPA) is a very comprehensive law enacted in the state of California in 2018. It is like GDPR in the sense that it dictates how companies are allowed to process the personal data of California citizens and their families. It also states which data is protected and details the requirements for protecting that data. This law also gives California residents a lot of control over the data collected by companies. Residents of California have the right to know what personal information is being collected, the option to decline the sale of said information, and the ability to request the deletion of their data. A company guilty of intentionally violating this law can be fined up to $7,500 per violation and $2,500 for an unintentional violation.

The Health Insurance Portability and Accountability Act (HIPAA) This federal law aims to protect patients' sensitive personal information, such as diagnosis, prescriptions, and lab results, from disclosure without consent or knowledge of the patient. An individual guilty of intentionally violating HIPAA can be fined up to $50,000 per violation and sentenced to up to one year of imprisonment. Companies should not aim to satisfy the minimum compliance requirements to avoid fines, as doing so will not improve their organizations' overall security. Instead, they should focus on improving their overall security posture, which will benefit them in the long run and position them as market leaders.

Data Minimization and Anonymization

There are some steps companies can take to secure our data and privacy.

Data Minimization

Data minimization is the principle that a company should only collect exactly what it needs to fulfill its specific purpose and retain the data for as long as necessary to provide the service. Let's look at an example. You downloaded a pizza ordering application on your phone, and during the installation, the app asks you to allow access to your location, camera, photos, and contacts. But wait, does it need to access your camera, photos, and contacts for you to order the pizza? A company that follows data minimization will only request access to your geolocation to deliver the pizza.

Data Anonymization

Anonymization is removing Personally Identifiable Information (PII) from the data set, making it impossible for the data to be linked to a specific person. This process is often used in software development or testing, where the company needs real data to test a product or to share the data with an external party that should not have access to the sensitive information. They will anonymize the data set before sharing it.

There are three ways to anonymize the data.

Data Masking: Data masking involves altering actual data to render it either valueless or fictitious. For instance, when you enter a password or log into a system, the characters you input might appear as dots or stars on the screen, illustrating data masking in action.

Data Pseudonymization: Pseudonymization replaces the original value with random ones. For example, a credit card number like 1232 5678 9101 1213 might be substituted with a random string like A2%ky86JL34x.

Tokenization: This method involves replacing sensitive data elements with unique tokens, such as account numbers or Social Security numbers. In the event of a data breach, these tokens lack meaningful information, preventing malicious actors from exploiting the compromised data. A token-generating tool securely stores a mapping of the original data, enhancing data protection, bolstering security, and safeguarding privacy.

Security and Privacy by Design

In most organizations, the mindset is that privacy is taken care of by the legal department or the compliance department, and cybersecurity takes care of securing the data. However, because of all those privacy laws, there is a new concept called Privacy by Design. That means during the product design phase, the product team, in collaboration with legal, compliance, and cyber, will work together to include controls that address privacy and security concerns during the product design phase. By doing so, they can quickly identify any potential problems that can affect privacy or security.

Privacy by Design Principles

Let's walk through the seven privacy principles.

1. **Proactive, not Reactive, Preventative, not Remedial:** This principle says that systems should be designed to prevent privacy risks from occurring in the first place instead of reacting to them after the fact.

2. **Privacy as the Default Setting**: Systems should protect the privacy of individuals when browsing the Internet or using an app, whether or not the user interacts with the settings. The default approach of any system should be to protect the user's privacy.

3. **Privacy Embedded into Design**: Privacy should be the primary design consideration when building a website, a software application, or a mobile app. Privacy should be the core requirement of the new system by design.

4. **Full Functionality - Positive Sum, not Zero-Sum:** Some argue that there must be a tradeoff between user experience and security if they have to include privacy. These folks have a zero-sum attitude. They should manifest a positive-sum attitude by working to integrate privacy into every design element with no tradeoffs.

5. **End-to-End Security - Lifecycle Protection:** Privacy by Design ensures security practices persist throughout the entire information life cycle, from when the users provide their personal information to when the data is destroyed. Security controls should be in place to protect the information's confidentiality, integrity, and availability.

6. **Visibility and Transparency - Keep it Open:** Organizations should handle and use this data according to the stated purposes. Having accessible and comprehensive policies and procedures that can be checked is an excellent way to show visibility and transparency.

7. **Respect for User Privacy - Keep it User-Centric:** In all decision-making, always keep the users' privacy in mind. Privacy is about protecting users' personal information.

Tips

Here are a couple of tips you can implement immediately to help protect your privacy.

1. Make sure you adjust the privacy settings of your social media accounts to limit who can see your posts and profile information online.

2. Check the privacy notice and the terms and conditions of companies you do business with to see what information they are collecting and what they intend to do with it so you can make an informed decision to allow or continue using their service.

Recap

We have addressed the vital topics of data privacy and security, highlighting the distinction between the two and the regulatory frameworks, such as GDPR, CCPA, and HIPAA, aimed at safeguarding sensitive information from misuse. We have examined the principles of security and privacy by design and their implications.

In Chapter 5, we will delve into personal cybersecurity controls individuals can implement to protect their personal information. We will cover topics such as creating strong passwords, using multi-factor authentication, being vigilant against phishing attacks, and securing your devices and networks. By the end of the next chapter, you will have a solid understanding of the steps you can take to safeguard your digital life.

Chapter 5:
Protecting Your Personal Information

The first part of this chapter will delve into the critical topic of password security and underscore the paramount importance of safeguarding both your data and privacy. We will explore the essential attributes of strong passwords and provide insights into leveraging tools to facilitate creating and managing strong passwords.

Understanding Password Security

Password security can be compared to having a door lock on your front door. If you buy an inexpensive one, it would be easy for someone to pick the lock and break into your house. But if you have a good one, it would be difficult for that person to break into your house. Creating unique and strong passwords is vital to keeping the bad guys away from your account or devices.

A password is a sequence or string of characters used to verify a user's identity, usually to gain access to a resource like a computer or an online banking account. Good passwords are essential in cybersecurity to prevent threat actors from gaining unauthorized access to your computer systems and networks.

Characteristics of Strong Passwords

Attackers employ various methods to gain unauthorized access to accounts, including password-based attacks. One common technique is the brute force attack, which involves trying numerous combinations until the correct password is discovered. Another approach is the password spraying attack, where attackers attempt commonly used passwords across multiple accounts to gain access. Using complex and unique passwords that are not reused can significantly enhance the security of your accounts.

To safeguard your accounts, it's essential to create passwords that are both long and complex. Opt for combinations of multiple words that are easy for you to remember but difficult for others to guess. A strong password should ideally be at least 12 characters long and include a mix of uppercase and lowercase letters, numbers, and special characters. Avoid using predictable information such as your date of birth, name, or pets' names. Refrain from using simple words like *princess* or *sunshine*, as these are easy targets for attackers.

You can employ mnemonic techniques to simplify the password-creation process. For example, try combining the first letter of each word from a phrase or a song you like with numbers and special characters. You can also use an online password generator tool to generate a complex password. Strong passwords can be challenging for many to recall, leading them to jot them down. However, one of the riskiest actions is storing all your passwords in one of those logbooks found on Amazon. Consider the potential consequences if such a logbook were lost or accessed by someone else. Instead, use a password manager. A password manager is software that will produce the passwords for you and, in one place, manage them. It uses a master password and two-factor authentication to secure access to all your passwords.

Another aspect of good password management revolves around your security questions to reset your passwords or recover your account. You need to treat them just like your password. Otherwise, someone can easily reset your password and take over your account. Most people share a ton of information on social media platforms, so if your security questions are about the high school you went to, the year you graduated, your mother's name, your first car, or your favorite football team, you need to change them right away to something else that only you would know.

Two-Factor Authentication (2FA)

Apart from passwords, another way of securing the accounts is through two-factor authentication (2FA), which is also commonly called two-step verification or dual-factor authentication. Two-factor authentication (2FA) is a security measure demanding the use of at least two forms of identification in order to gain access to a system. When you login to your bank account online and enter your password, you are often asked to type a one-time password (OTP) that was sent to your cellular device or email. This additional measure (second step of authentication, 2FA) helps increase the security of your account during signing in.

Two-factor authentication (2FA) typically involves two types of credentials for added security. The first factor is something you know, such as a password, PIN, or the answer to a security question. The second factor is something you have, like a security token, smartphone, or ID card. Alternatively, it can also be an inherent factor, such as your fingerprint or facial recognition, used to access or unlock your device.

If a website or system requires you to enter both your password and PIN, it doesn't qualify as two-factor authentication. This is because it relies on the same type of authentication, which is something you know. Another example of the 2FA is when you get cash out of an

ATM. The ATM will prompt you for your bank card or credit card. That's something you have and possess, and then it will ask you for your pin, which you know. That is 2-factor authentication.

Two-Factor Authentication Methods

As mentioned earlier, achieving 100% security is challenging in the realm of cybersecurity. Similarly, certain 2FA methods we'll discuss have vulnerabilities that attackers can target. Organizations often integrate two or more of these methods to enhance security measures, making it more challenging for malicious actors to compromise an account.

OneTime Code: Usually, they will send the code to your email or your phone, or you will receive a voice call, and they will provide you with the code, which you will enter on the screen. By sending the code to either your phone or email or calling you, the company is verifying that you are the owner of the account and that you own the device or the account that you have registered during the enrollment process. The issue with that method is that if a user used a weak password, a bad actor could have easily taken over the account. The malicious actor would be the one receiving the code, defeating the purpose of 2FA, which is to secure the account. Criminals, sometimes pretending to be customers, can get mobile phone companies to transfer the victim's phone number to a new SIM card, thus gaining access to the onetime code.

Authenticator Apps: Authenticator apps such as Google Authenticator or Microsoft Authenticator will generate a onetime code that you will use to enter during the sign-in process. You will install the authenticator app on your phone, so it will always be with you, and you don't need phone service for the authenticator to work. It is a better option than the previous ones we discussed, as the secret key is stored on your phone and cannot be intercepted.

Biometric Authentication: Biometric authentication, whether fingerprint scanning, facial recognition, or iris scanning, offers users both convenience and a higher level of security compared to passwords. Biometric data is usually stored on the device to enhance security and protect user privacy. Storing this information locally means it remains within the user's control, reducing the risk of exposure to potential breaches or unauthorized access. By keeping biometric data on the device it minimizes the chances of it being intercepted or accessed by external parties, ensuring a higher level of data protection. Sophisticated attackers may compromise biometric systems.

Hardware Security Keys: Hardware security keys are also known as Universal Second Factor (U2F) or YubiKeys. They are hardware security keys that you will plug into your computer or phone. Those keys provide a second factor or additional security to your 2FA method. The methods we discussed earlier only verify the user's identity, not the specific online platform or application they're accessing. This can leave accounts vulnerable to man-in-the-middle attacks. During setup, a hardware security key exchanges unique information with the online platform or application. When a user tries to log in later, the platform sends a specific request to the key, which will only grant access if the request matches the pre-shared information.

YubiKeys, or universal hardware security keys, have been around since 2007. Some people like to use them instead of the software version of Google Authenticator or Microsoft Authenticator. They are not too expensive. You can find one for $25 online, and it is recommended to have a backup plan in case you lose your YubiKey. The backup plan can be to turn on 2FA on your mobile devices using Microsoft Authenticator or Google Authenticator.

A significant drawback of using 2FA, YubiKeys, or hardware security keys is that if the key uses a USB-A port, it may not work with your Android device, your iPhone, or an older model of your MacBook Pro without purchasing an adapter. YubiKeys are very easy to use. You plug it into your computer's USB port or use a wireless key supporting Near Field Communication (NFC). When prompted, you need to push the key button, which will allow you to authenticate into your account.

Advantages and Limitations of 2FA

Two-factor authentication offers several advantages, such as increased security against password attacks and protection against phishing attacks even if the user was tricked into revealing their password. Without the second factor, the malicious actor won't be able to take over their account. However, it is essential to be aware of its limitations, such as the need for a backup option in case you lose access to the primary 2FA method. If you lose your key, you may be locked out of your account forever if you don't have a backup plan.

2FA can give you a false sense of security. Users may become complacent and assume that having 2FA enabled means their accounts are secure, leading them to overlook other security best practices, such as using strong, unique passwords and keeping software up to date. Also, a malicious actor who can take over your account can use 2FA against you. That is why it is crucial to protect your accounts by practicing good security hygiene.

Safe Internet Browsing and Email Practices

The Internet presents numerous cybersecurity risks, making it imperative to prioritize safe online practices to defend against malware, phishing attempts, and other threats. In this section, we will teach you how to distinguish between safe and malicious websites and share precautions to help you avoid falling prey to phishing attacks and cybercrimes.

Recognizing Secure Websites and Phishing Websites

Your computer can be a treasure trove of information for hackers, making it crucial to protect yourself. Hackers employ various tactics, such as enticing you to visit compromised websites to infect your computer and steal your personal information. In the past, the absence of a green padlock in the URL indicated the site was susceptible to data breaches and that malicious actors could intercept your sensitive information. With malicious actors now utilizing SSL encryption, it is no longer a reliable indicator.

The green padlock means the site has a security certificate, and your connection is encrypted from your browser to the website server. So your communication is not in clear text, and if someone sniffs the traffic, they can't read the information. However, if you are connected to a malicious website, it does not mean that your information will be safe.

When a website uses encryption, you will see *HTTPS* in the URL address. If it is not, you will see *HTTP*, which means your connection to the server is not encrypted. And if you type your username and password, anyone sniffing on the communication can see your credentials and all discussions with the server in clear text. Sometimes, you will see the ability to add an exception even though the website is not using a secure connection. Don't do it unless you absolutely know what you are doing. If someone that you don't even know tells you in an email to click on a link and add an exception to an unsecured website, don't do that either. They are tricking you into revealing your sensitive information for fraud or to take over your account.

We will cover the nine steps you can follow to check if the website you are visiting is safe and to protect yourself. But keep in mind, not one step by itself will tell you either way. Use at least several of these steps.

1. **Check for the *https://* or the padlock.** Even though HTTPS doesn't mean the website is safe. However, it is an indication that the

website you are on is protecting your communications. By the end of 2023, Google Chrome no longer shows the padlock icon because HTTPS is becoming a standard, so you will need to follow the other steps below to ensure the website is safe.

2. **Check the domain name.** There are a couple of reasons you need to do that. Cybercriminals often create domain names and websites that are almost identical to deceive users into believing that the website is affiliated with or endorsed by a legitimate brand. The malicious actor may register *walmart-deals.com* instead of *walmart.com* to trick users into thinking they are visiting an official website offering special deals or promotions. These types of domains are called cousin domains.

Another reason to check the domain name is because of a type of phishing attack called typo squatting. With typo squatting, the attacker targets people who accidentally mistype a website address. They will register a website with a similar name to trick them into visiting the fake website to steal their information. They guess what spelling errors people will probably make, and then they will purchase that domain name. To protect yourself, it is essential to double-check the spelling and the URL address to ensure it is correct. Also, bookmark the websites you visit often. If you are doing a Google search for a company, the first three to four results at the top are typically advertisements, but if you scroll down, you will find the company name you are looking for.

3. **Check the visual appearance of the website**. Does the website look strange? Does it look unprofessional or choppy? Does it have misspelled words? Lately, however, with ChatGPT and other AI tools, malicious actors have been able to build excellent websites without grammatical errors. So you still need to be careful and not only use this step alone to identify a safe website.

4. **Look for the contact information**. Look for how to contact the company. Is their phone number, location, or physical address in a

country you can trust? If in doubt, Google is your best friend. Do a Google search to see if the company is legitimate. If they have a phone number, call them. See if you can talk to someone.

5. **Check out the history of the website.** There's an online digital archive called the Wayback Machine, run by a nonprofit organization that has been around since 1996. This website allows you to see how long a website has been created. What did it look like, and if anything has changed recently? This way, you can see if something fishy is going on, as malicious actors may have purchased the domain recently because it expired. That domain may have had some traffic back in the day. They are trying to use that same address to trick people into visiting their website. You can go to archive.org to use that tool.

6. **Check the privacy notice.** Privacy notices tell you what information the website or the organization will collect and what they will do with that personal information. You should be very careful if a website lacks a privacy notice.

7. **Check the ownership of the website.** You can check who owns the website by going to https://lookup.icann.org to confirm the ownership of the website. Confirming the website's actual owners will help you verify its legitimacy. However, note that many websites hosted by major organizations or even individuals may use the privacy option when registering domain names to prevent being bombarded with spam or to protect themselves against cybercriminals. If you are uncomfortable providing sensitive information to them, don't.

8. **Use endpoint protection software, such as anti-malware software.** It is impossible with the naked eye to know if a website is running malicious code or has a reputation for being malicious. Cybercriminals can exploit security flaws in popular websites to infect their visitors. That is why purchasing anti-malware software

that will block malicious websites and drive-by downloads is advisable.

9. **Use good judgment.** Based on your activities on the website, consider if it's requesting sensitive information that seems inappropriate or out of place. Are you prompted to pay for a product using bank transfers or cryptocurrency instead of a credit card? Are there promises of a high return on investment or deals that appear too good to be true? Consider twice before providing your data or continuing to use the site in such situations.

Browser Security Settings

For optimal protection While browsing the internet, it's important to familiarize yourself with the security settings of your modern browser. These browsers have security filters designed to alert you about harmful websites and other security risks. For example, Microsoft Edge uses Microsoft Defender SmartScreen. The Defender SmartScreen will check the website you are visiting against a list of reported phishing attempts. It will block the website and let you know if it is a match. In addition, Defender SmartScreen will check your downloads against a list of reported malicious software sites and programs known to be unsafe.

Google Chrome and Mozilla Firefox also have security features, and some are turned on by default, but for others, you have to turn them on. It is essential, however, to keep your browsers up-to-date if you want to benefit from the security features. A second layer of protection is obtained by downloading add-ons, such as the Web of Trust.

Phishing and Social Engineering Awareness

In the second part of this chapter, we will concentrate on raising awareness about phishing and social engineering. These deceptive tactics are widespread in the cyber-realm, posing threats to individuals and organizations. Therefore, it is crucial to grasp the strategies that can shield you and your organization from falling prey to their schemes. Let's delve into ways to ensure your safety.

Understanding Phishing and Social Engineering

Social engineering is a type of attack where the malicious actor will use psychological manipulation to trick you into making security mistakes or giving away sensitive information, such as passwords, banking information, or credit card information. They can target you either via email, text, or phone call. The threat actors can be anywhere in the world.

Their objectives can be to steal your money, your personal information, commit identity theft, corporate espionage, or even sabotage a company. When they attack you over email, it is called a phishing attack. Phishing is a subcategory of social engineering where the malicious actor will send an email to get you to act, such as downloading a file or going to a link where they can collect your credentials or personal information. They can also use you to gain access to your corporate network. Let's cover some common methods of social engineering attacks.

Social Engineering Techniques

Social engineering techniques rely heavily on human psychology to work.

Pretexting is a very common technique used by malicious actors. In pretexting, the attacker crafts a convincing story to manipulate the victim into divulging information. These malicious actors often scour social media to gather details about the victim, aiming to build trust and extract further information during their interactions.

Baiting: Baiting means attracting the victims using some kind of reward (e.g., a job offer or attractive promotion) in exchange for the completion of a simple action. They use social networking sites like Facebook, Instagram, or Twitter, malicious ads promoting huge discounts for special offers or an attachment with an enticing name, such as executive compensation, dirty pictures of a celebrity, etc. They will also infect USB flash drives with malware and place them at strategic points where potential victims will be bound to find these devices. The virus installs itself immediately after the infected flash drive is connected to the PC.

Tailgating or Piggybacking: Tailgating is used to gain physical access to protected areas or a building. The tailgater will wait for an authorized user to open the door in the secure area and will follow right behind him. They can also impersonate a delivery driver or a custodian worker to gain access to the building.

Scareware: The victim will be bombarded with pop-up messages containing fictitious malware or viruses found on their computers. They will be provided with a phone number to call technical support, and during the conversation, they will be prompted to pay for fake or simulated malware removal software.

Honeytrap: A honeytrap involves luring individuals, typically men, into engaging with seemingly attractive female profiles, often fictitious, to coax them into disclosing sensitive information. This can lead to financial theft or compromise their company's security.

Phishing Attacks

Phishing is a mix of different attacks, some of which include email phishing, vishing, smishing, and angler phishing. Phishing emails will present some characteristics, such as a sense of urgency to log in to your account immediately or take action. They can ask you to transfer money or acknowledge that you have received a refund from the government, but sometimes they will have an attachment that you will need to open to edit.

Types of Phishing Attacks

We will cover some of the different phishing attacks.

Spear phishing: Spear phishing is a targeted, customized version of phishing, where the malicious actor will go after a specific person or a group, like a system administrator or a government employee, intending to get them to reveal sensitive information. The bad actor will research as much information as possible about the target, what he likes, his shopping habits, and his reading habits; all that information can be found on social media. This way, he can customize the email for that individual.

Whaling: Whaling specifically aims at high-ranking executives such as CEOs and CFOs, as they typically hold access to sensitive trade secrets and valuable information. The objective of whaling attacks is often to steal confidential information, gain unauthorized access to systems, or perpetrate a financial fraud by impersonating influential figures within an organization.

Business Email Compromise (BEC): BEC happens when a bad actor compromises the email account of one of the executives, such as the financial officer, to trick other business partners, employees, or customers into transferring money to a bad actor's account or purchasing gift cards to send to them.

The bad actor will monitor the email activity of the executive to understand his behavior, business processes, and procedures before crafting his email. Once he has the information, he will craft an email that sounds like it comes from the executive. In that email, he will have an urgent request from the executive to his assistant, the employee, or the business partner, requesting them to wire money to an external account, which the malicious actor owns.

Angler Phishing: Angler phishing is a recent tactic whereby the malicious actor fabricates a false social media profile, posing as a customer service representative of a company, to exploit disgruntled consumers and coax them into disclosing sensitive information.

Vishing: This is a type of attack that is done via a phone call. The bad actor typically calls the victim, claiming they're from Microsoft, PayPal, or Amazon. They have noticed suspicious activities on the victim's computer or their PayPal account. They will ask them to verify their bank account, credit card, or other personally identifiable information that they will use to commit identity fraud or financial fraud.

Smishing, or text message phishing: In SMS attacks, the attacker uses text messages to trick individuals into revealing sensitive information or performing specific actions, such as clicking on malicious links or providing personal information. For instance, an individual receives a text message claiming to be from their bank, stating that there has been suspicious activity on their account and urging them to click on a link to verify their account details. However, the link takes the user to a fake website designed to steal login credentials and other personal information.

Protecting Against Phishing

Here are some tips on protecting yourself against phishing attacks.

Avoid clicking on suspicious links or downloading attachments from unknown sources. Ask yourself if you requested this information or if you started this communication. If not, don't click on the link or download the attachment. If the email's sender pretends to represent a company that you know, look up the number online and call the company to verify that it's legit. Even if you know the sender, always confirm they have sent you the email or the attachment because their email could have been compromised, and now the attacker is using it to spread their malware.

Follow this checklist.

- Double-check the email address and the URL for any discrepancies.

- If they represent a bank, does the email address say gmail.com or hotmail.com? Or does it have your bank's name?

- If they request you click the link or download an attachment like an invoice, be very wary.

- Do they warn you of any negative consequences if the request is incomplete?

- Are they saying they noticed suspicious activity or log-in attempts on your account?

- Does the email have a vague signature or no signature at all?

- Is the email directly addressed to you, or does it say *dear sir*, *dear customer*, or *dear ma'am*?

- Do they request you enter your credentials or financial information to verify an order you have placed?

Be skeptical about phone scams when you receive a call from a stranger or if you did not start the communication. Be cautious about sharing sensitive information. If they say they represent a vendor and ask you for personal information, tell them you will call them back and go to the vendor's website or call the vendor to confirm their claim.

As an additional layer to protect you against social engineering attacks, it is vital to use a different password for each account besides two-factor authentication.

Email Filters and Spam Protection

According to a report from Deloitte, 91% of all cyberattacks begin with a phishing email, underscoring the vital need for companies to fortify their defenses. To empower their workforce against such threats, many organizations offer security awareness training and conduct simulated phishing exercises. These measures ensure employees can swiftly recognize and report suspicious emails to the cybersecurity team.

Businesses employ email filtering tools to diminish the influx of spam and harmful emails. These filters scan both incoming and outgoing emails, categorizing them based on specific tags like spam, bulk, adult content, and potential viruses. While this filtering process significantly curtails the number of undesirable and malicious emails, it's not entirely flawless. Occasionally, it might erroneously block genuine emails or permit malicious ones to pass. Hence, it's paramount for users to remain vigilant, scrutinizing both the email address and its content to avoid clicking on malicious links. Regularly reviewing the spam folder ensures authentic emails aren't mistakenly flagged as spam.

Tips

Here are some additional measures to safeguard yourself against phishing attacks:

1. If you are utilizing Firefox, enabling *Deceptive Content and Dangerous Software Protection* mode combined with two-factor authentication (2FA) would be highly recommended for the online safety of your accounts.

2. Maintaining a clean social media presence is crucial. Malicious actors often scour the internet for personal information, making it essential to regularly review and sanitize your social media accounts. Minimizing the amount of personal data available reduces the risk of falling victim to spear phishing attacks.

3. Avoid connecting unknown USB drives to your computer, especially if you find them lying around or aren't certain about their origin. Malicious individuals often preload these drives with malware and deliberately leave them in public areas, hoping

unsuspecting people will plug them in, compromising their computers.

4. Finally, make sure you periodically backup your data. In the unfortunate case of a malware or phishing attack infecting your system, having backups stored on an external hard drive or cloud storage platform such as Dropbox, OneDrive, or Google Drive ensures a secure duplicate of your data for recovery.

Recap

This chapter focused on maintaining strong password security. We highlighted the necessity of protecting personal data through effective password practices and outlined the characteristics of robust passwords. We introduced tools designed to aid in secure password creation and management. The chapter also explored the role of two-factor authentication (2FA) in enhancing account security, discussing various 2FA methods, best practices, and implementation guidance. While recognizing the advantages of 2FA, we also addressed its limitations. We covered safe internet browsing habits and concluded with insights into phishing attacks and preventative measures to avoid becoming a victim.

In Chapter 6, we will cover malware and software vulnerabilities and the importance of regular updates and patching. We'll talk about antivirus and anti-malware software to protect your personal devices.

Chapter 6:
Understanding and Managing Threats: Viruses, Malware, Countermeasures, and Vulnerability Management

In this chapter, we delve into the world of cybersecurity threats, focusing on viruses and malware, their impacts, and origins. We then transition to proactive countermeasures like antivirus software and advanced threat detection systems. The chapter emphasizes vulnerability management, highlighting the importance of identifying and mitigating system vulnerabilities to enhance cybersecurity. Readers will gain insights into essential tools and strategies for defending against evolving cyber threats.

Virus and Malware Overview

The first malware originated from an experimental program created by Bob Thomas while he was working on the ARPANET network for BBN, now known as Raytheon BBN Technologies. The program aimed to transfer data between two mainframe computers running the TNext operating system. However, the program malfunctioned, causing corruption in the mainframe computers and displaying the famous message, *I am the Creeper. Catch me if you can*. Unlike present-day computer viruses, the program was created with no malicious intent. Ray Tomlinson, who was also working on the ARPANET network, later enhanced the program code to enable it to replicate itself instead of merely transferring between computers. This led to the self-replicating version of the Creeper program being recognized as the first computer virus. Subsequently, Tomlinson developed another program, named the Reaper, to eradicate the Creeper virus, establishing it as the first antivirus program.

Malware refers to a range of harmful software designed to compromise computer systems. The motivations behind these malicious programs differ depending on the threat actor's objectives. Some aim to hijack computer resources for cryptocurrency mining, while others focus on espionage or fraud by stealing sensitive data. Some malware sabotages or destroys computer systems for political reasons or to extort money through ransomware attacks.

Let's explore several common families of malware.

Spyware: As the name suggests, it is malware that spies on you, collects sensitive information, and can even create remote access for the bad actor. A specific type of spyware is called a keylogger, which records your keystrokes to collect your passwords, banking information, and other sensitive information without your knowledge and will send the information to the bad actor.

Adware: This malicious software will collect your web surfing habits and provide related advertisements to you. It can change your browser's homepage and redirect your browser to a malicious site to download Trojan viruses.

Ransomware: Ransomware is scareware that encrypts the files on your computer and then demands you pay a ransom to regain access to them. Ransomware is commonly used as part of a phishing campaign, and once you, as the user, click on the malicious link, it will download the ransomware into your system. A well-known malware attack was the WannaCry ransomware attack in May 2017. The threat actors encrypted files on hundreds of thousands of computers in over 150 countries and demanded payment to unlock them. Businesses, hospitals, and government agencies were affected by the WannaCry ransomware attack, resulting in billions of dollars in damages.

Signs of Malware Infection

A typical sign is that your computer is running slower than usual or crashing frequently. You may also see pop-up ads or other unwanted messages on your screen. You may notice strange files or programs you did not install on your computer. Other things you may notice are:

- Your web browser is redirecting you to unfamiliar or suspicious websites.

- Your computer is behaving unexpectedly, such as opening or closing programs.

- Your antivirus software may report malware infections or block access to specific websites.

- You can also receive strange and threatening messages from unknown sources.

- Your friends or colleagues may report to you they are receiving spam, or you can see in your sent items that mass emails are being sent to your contacts.

Computer Viruses

Computer viruses represent a distinct category within the broader spectrum of malware. When executed, they will replicate themselves. They can modify files or other programs on your computer and even delete the operating system files. Computer viruses are like real-life viruses. They need host and user interaction to replicate.

There are several ways you can catch a virus. You can get a virus by downloading infected files like a Word document or by downloading pirated music and movies off the Internet. The virus remains dormant even as you download the infected files, waiting for activation once the user executes the tainted file or program. Upon infecting your computer, it may delete files, disrupt other programs, spread to other computers on the network, steal passwords, record keystrokes, inundate your email with spam, or hijack your system to form a bot network, depending on the intended purpose for which it was designed.

Types of Computer Viruses

Worm: A computer worm is a type of malware that replicates itself and spreads to other computers and networks independently. Unlike viruses, worms don't need to attach themselves to an existing program or file to spread. It does it automatically by exploiting program vulnerabilities in the operating system to spread from computer to computer on a network and even over the Internet.

Trojan viruses: Trojan viruses are named after the epic story of how the Greeks circumvented the Trojan defense using a deceitful Trojan horse and ultimately capture Troy. These viruses disguise themselves as harmless files or software in order to mislead users into pressing the DOWNLOAD button. Sometimes, without your notice, you may just end up bringing Trojans through the installation of seemingly harmless magnifier apps and website plugins or accessing pirated movies online. Cybercriminals develop special Trojans with numerous malicious goals. For example, Trojans such as banker Trojans aim at stealing all of your banking and credit card data, and other Trojans such as the Mail Finder Trojan obtain email addresses from the infected device. Besides, Game Thief Trojans take actions for hacking game players' accounts aimed at the theft of their gaming accounts. Being notorious, it is necessary for us to be extra cautious and alert in order to remain untouched by Trojan horses.

Macro-viruses: A macrovirus is a computer virus written in a macro language found in software applications like Microsoft Office (e.g., Word, Excel, and PowerPoint). These languages enable users to automate tasks with custom scripts, enhancing workflow and automating repetitive actions. These viruses spread through Excel sheets, Word documents, and any software that uses macros. Malicious actors usually use email attachments as the attack vector to spread macroviruses.

Antivirus and Anti-Malware Software

In today's digital age, malware is a serious threat to both home PCs and enterprise IT systems. To tackle these malicious threats, specialized software, such as anti-malware and antivirus programs, have been created. These sophisticated tools work hard to detect and remove malicious software, assuring the safety and security of your digital environment.

How Antimalware Functions

Anti-malware software relies on complex detection and protection mechanisms. Below are the common methods used for detection:

Definition-Base: This strategy utilizes a comprehensive list of identified malicious files. By comparing harmful files to this blacklist, anti-malware tools can quickly identify and flag any matches, subsequently removing or quarantining the detected files. identify and flag any matches, subsequently removing or quarantining the detected files.

Heuristic: The heuristic strategy is used to identify new forms of malicious software (malware) that haven't been previously detected or classified. Instead of relying solely on known signatures of malware, heuristic analysis focuses on the behavior and characteristics of suspicious files or programs. By analyzing how a file behaves or operates, heuristic analysis can determine if it's harmful.

Sandboxing: Sandboxing is a valuable tool in the arsenal of anti-malware solutions. This approach entails executing questionable applications within a secure, isolated environment offered by anti-malware programs. By observing the behavior of an application or file in this controlled setting, anti-malware software can determine if it poses a threat. If the program shows signs of malicious activity, the measures are taken to eliminate the risk. Conversely, if the file behaves safely, it is permitted to function outside of the sandbox without restrictions.

Machine Learning and Artificial Intelligence: The rapid advancement of machine learning and artificial intelligence has revolutionized malware defense strategies. Leveraging these sophisticated technologies, anti-malware programs can efficiently process vast amounts of data, identifying patterns and classifying software as either malicious or harmless. This automated method enhances both the speed and precision of threat detection, providing an additional safeguard for your digital resources.

When malware is detected, anti-malware software typically responds by automatically deleting the infected files. However, in some rare cases, deleting the malicious file could harm your computer. To mitigate this risk, anti-malware products have a quarantine feature. This feature isolates infected files, keeping them separate to prevent further damage.

Antivirus software works on the same principles as anti-malware, thoroughly examining your computer's memory and files for any traces of dangerous code or files. When the antivirus program detects a threat, it immediately deletes or quarantines it, protecting your computer or mobile device from potential harm. Some powerful antivirus applications even contain a host intrusion prevention system, which continually monitors your system for unusual changes and activities, offering an additional layer of protection.

What is the difference between antivirus and anti-malware? Antivirus usually deals with older, more established threats, such as worms, viruses, and Trojans. Anti-malware focuses on newer threats such as spyware and malware, delivered by zero-day exploits.

Choosing the Right Software

Anti-malware and Trojan software are essential cybersecurity tools. They detect, prevent, and remove malicious software such as viruses, worms, Trojans, and spyware. They act like a defense barrier; scan and monitor your devices for any signs of suspicious activity. Therefore, it is crucial to choose the right antivirus solution for your system.

When selecting an antivirus or anti-malware solution, consider specific criteria to ensure you choose a reputable vendor. For many, especially those who frequently use the internet and email, opting for a reliable security solution is crucial for safer online activities. Here's a short list.

Check Reviews: Check the reliability of the software by reading the reviews, as some antivirus and anti-malware can be useless and let malware into your systems. Some software can conflict with other programs on your computer or may not work with the operating system, like a Mac OS, which may lead to malfunction or shutdown of the antivirus software altogether. Personal copies of malware software will scan your computer at regular intervals, but in the enterprise environment, they usually schedule the scan to prevent slowness or frustration for the users.

Software Updates: The right software often offers regular updates to protect against emerging threats, ensuring that your digital environment remains secure.

Benefits of Using Antivirus and Anti-Malware

Having anti-malware doesn't mean you can be careless, so avoiding suspicious websites and pirated software downloads and exercising caution with email attachments are crucial. Running an antivirus and anti-malware program can have several benefits. Such as:

- Providing real-time protection by continuously monitoring your computer.

- During the booting process, it will scan the boot files to ensure you don't have a boot sector virus.

- It will scan individual files on your computer to detect malware.

- It will protect your sensitive information by blocking malicious websites, phishing scams, and by scanning incoming and outgoing emails for malicious attachment.

- It restores infected files to their previous state..

- Has a firewall that monitors incoming and outgoing network traffic and blocks potential cyberattacks.

- It scans USB drives and any external hard drive to ensure they don't have any viruses or malware.

- Improves the performance of the computer by terminating unused programs and background processes that can slow it down.

Software Updates, Patching, and Patch Management

This section discusses the need to update your software regularly, emphasizing its vital role in resolving vulnerabilities and strengthening cyberattack defenses. We will discuss the patch management process and provide recommendations for its implementation. Finally, we will discuss the differences between automated and manual updates.

Importance of Software Updates

Many people like to delay software updates because they think it will take too much of their time, and sometimes they don't want to restart their browser or the computer because they are too busy. Are you one of them? We hope you will change your opinion after hearing the information we are about to share. Timely software updates are crucial for several reasons.

1. **New Features**: It is common for software to receive new enhancements to keep up with rapid changes in the industry. There will be new features or something more efficient with the improvements. It is usually good when the software manufacturer wants to give you the latest product version, as Apple does with its products.

2. **Bug Fixes:** Another reason for software updates is for bug fixes, which improve software stability and performance. Something

within the software product may not work correctly, but it has been fixed. It may not be something you have seen or may not be evident to you. However, these flaws may only manifest themselves under specific conditions. It is important to apply the update when the vendor releases it.

3. **Security Enhancements:** Because software is so complex, we have bugs that can impact the functionality and security of the application or the software. Depending on the software security flaw, it could cause your personal data to be compromised or even allow attackers to take over your computer. Hackers know how to look for unpatched and vulnerable systems online.

Those are the primary reasons you should always want to keep your software up-to-date. Yes, these notifications can be annoying, especially when you are in the middle of something. However, installing the updates and rebooting your system can make the difference between a few minutes of downtime and getting your system hacked and your information stolen.

Patch Management

Let's discuss the process for keeping your software up-to-date in the corporate environment. Patch management is part of applying software updates to keep your computer systems and network secure. It also helps keep an organization compliant with security and privacy regulations, such as HIPAA and PCI DSS.

You may ask, what is a patch? A patch is a modification to a program to improve its security, performance, or functionality.

Patch management involves identifying necessary updates for systems, acquiring these patches, testing them in a controlled environment to identify any conflicts or potential issues, and finally, installing them to ensure optimal system performance and security.

Implementing a patch Program in your Organization

Here are the critical steps of a patch management process:

1. **Have a Patch Management Policy**: The policy will provide the governance to enforce the requirement that all systems and software must be patched and updated promptly.

2. **Asset Inventory:** You will need an inventory of your devices, operating systems, and apps that must be patched and grouped by criticality.

3. **Standardize Systems and Operating System Versions and Types**: This will allow the company to patch its system faster and more efficiently when they are grouped by operating systems based on version and type. To illustrate, you can patch all your Windows servers on Saturday night, your Linux systems on Sunday night, and all your Windows desktop computers on Monday night.

4. **Vulnerabilities Prioritization:** The organization needs to prioritize its vulnerabilities by criticality because of limited time. The ever-changing threat landscape and insufficient staff prioritization help an organization secure its most critical assets by patching them first and then the less critical assets.

5. **Testing:** Testing patches within a segregated environment guarantees their security when implemented in production, safeguarding mission-critical applications. The security team will conduct thorough validation to ensure the patch effectively fixes the identified flaw before deployment.

6. **Running a Pilot:** Running a pilot of patches on a sample of devices will give the company a second chance to detect issues that did not appear during the lab testing.

7. **Rescan the Environment:** Rescanning the environment is essential to confirm the installation of patches and identify any that are still missing.

8. **Do a Phase Rollout:** Patching in phases is crucial for effective risk and resource management. It allows organizations to identify potential issues in a controlled manner, minimizing disruptions to operations.

9. **Documenting:** The organization should maintain records of system vulnerabilities both before and after applying patches, along with corresponding test results. This documentation helps identify if a patch has introduced any issues. Having these records on hand demonstrates compliance during audits, showcasing consistent system patching efforts.

Companies can minimize their attack surface through effective patch management and enhance overall cybersecurity defenses.

Automatic Updates vs Manual Updates

Which method should an organization choose for patching? The decision between automatic and manual updates isn't universal; it varies based on the organization's specific needs. Factors to consider include the criticality of business systems or applications in use and the acceptable downtime. Compatibility between a security patch and an application or system can pose challenges, emphasizing the importance of testing patches before deploying them in a production environment.

What are the benefits of automatic updates? Automatic updates are best for security fixes that address system vulnerabilities. Once a security vulnerability has been resolved and patched by the software manufacturer, it is automatically installed on your system, so you are good to go.

Automatic updates are also ideal for operating system updates that have been fully tested. Automatic updates can easily be reverted if something goes wrong.

Manual updates, on the other hand, are useful for things like firmware, BIOS, and network switches or routers. They are also suitable for systems and servers that are critical for business operations. Business-critical systems cannot afford to be down, so manual updates would be best in this circumstance. Whichever approach you choose, it is vital to be consistent with your patching.

Tips

Here are a couple of practical tips that you can implement right away.

1. Install reputable antivirus and anti-malware software on all your devices. Run regular scans to detect and remove any malicious software that may have infiltrated your system.

2. Enable automatic updates for your device's operating system and apps to ensure you have the latest security patches. Regularly check for updates if automatic updates are not an option for the device or software.

Recap

We began this chapter by exploring the origins of the first computer virus and the evolution of antivirus solutions. We delved into various types of malware and viruses, as well as the functionality of anti-malware tools. We discussed a prevalent approach organizations adopt to address vulnerabilities: patch management.

In the upcoming Chapter 7, we will discuss strategies to safeguard your home network. We'll explore methods to enhance the security of your router devices and share configuration best practices suitable for individuals and organizations to defend against cyber threats.

Chapter 7:
Wi-Fi and IoT Defense Strategies for Individuals and Enterprises

In today's interconnected world, ensuring the security of our digital assets is paramount. This chapter delves into comprehensive strategies tailored for both individuals and enterprises to fortify their Wi-Fi networks and safeguard IoT devices. We will explore the intricacies of home network security, emphasizing best practices to thwart unauthorized access and potential breaches. As the Internet of Things (IoT) becomes increasingly prevalent in our daily lives, we'll discuss how to secure these interconnected devices to prevent vulnerabilities. Whether you're safeguarding your personal devices or managing security across an enterprise network, this chapter offers actionable insights to bolster your defenses.

Secure Wi-Fi Practices

This section dives into the realm of secure Wi-Fi practices, emphasizing measures to safeguard your wireless network from unauthorized access. We will elucidate the importance of securing your Wi-Fi network and outline the essential configurations necessary to shield yourself from online threats.

Understanding Wi-Fi Security

Do you recall when accessing the Internet meant connecting to a neighbor's Wi-Fi without having it at home? Many of us resorted to this practice, although it wasn't the most ethical choice. However, using a neighbor's wireless connection can expose them to potential risks. If a malicious attacker exploits this connection for illegal activities, the IP address will be traced back to the unsuspecting neighbor's residence. An IP address is a unique address to identify a device on the Internet or a network, like your street address. Things have changed. Even the most modern routers now come with security features by default. However, as the consumer, you must customize it based on your needs.

Malicious hackers are opportunistic and will go after the easy target first, as many people don't know how to secure their routers or networks. Since COVID, the home has become the office for most people, so as cybersecurity professionals, whether we work from home, in the coffee shop, or in the office, security should be at the top of our priority list. Some of you deal with company-sensitive data or its customers. How will you protect your organization and these customers while working at home? At the end of this section, you will know what you need to do.

Threats to Home Network

There are a few threats to the home network that you need to be aware of.

Inbound Attack: A malicious actor can gain unauthorized access to your home Wi-Fi network and attack your other devices, such as your smart TV, computers, and tablets. This type of attack is called an inbound attack, and the objective is to steal sensitive information or spy on you.

Outbound Attack: This is where the malicious actor uses your network to commit crimes, execute malware attacks on your other devices, or use your network for distributed denial of service (DDoS) attacks.

Sniffing Attack: They can also launch a sniffing attack on your network. A sniffing attack is when the malicious actor is on your network and is passively sniffing the communication between your computer and other devices inside or outside your network. The communication is not encrypted via TLS or a secure socket layer. That communication is in clear text, and they will collect your credentials.

Man-In-The-Middle Attack: A man-in-the-middle attack is very active, where the malicious actor places himself between the communication. For example, if you connect to your bank to make a transaction online instead of talking directly to your bank, the attacker is in the middle of that conversation. That is why it's called a man-in-the-middle attack. He will receive the information you're sending to your bank server, modify it, and then pass it on the server. Once he gets a response from the server, he will modify the information again before passing it to you. If you transfer $100, he will change it to something like $10,000. Then, he will change the bank account information to transfer it to his bank account. As you can see, this type of attack is very dangerous, and we will show you how you can protect your home network to prevent that from happening.

Advanced Wi-Fi Network Hardening Techniques

Here are some proactive steps you can take to secure your home router.

Change the Default Settings: The first thing you need to do to protect your network is to change the default username and password of your Wi-Fi router. Routers come with default usernames and passwords and a Service Set Identifier (SSID). The service set identifier, or SSID, is the name of your network. The default password is known to everyone. If you search the Internet, you will find a list of default usernames and passwords for the most widely purchased home routers. SSIDs might be unique to a certain brand, like Linksys or Netgear. Changing your default SSID to something different makes it a little difficult for the malicious actor in your vicinity to recognize which wireless router you are using. This is called security through obscurity. In full candor, changing your network SSID won't work for a professional and determined bad actor, as he can use sophisticated tools out there.

Another thing to note is that anytime you reset your router to factory default, it will reset your password and the SSID back to factory default. You will need to modify them again.

Turn off Wi-Fi-protected setup (WPS): While not all routers offer this feature, many include the WPS option, which streamlines connecting wireless devices to your network. It works by hitting a button called WPS on the router, which will allow devices to connect with no password. If your router is in an area that is accessible, it might be a good idea to turn off the WPS capability in the management panel to prevent the bad actor from having access to your network.

Turn on the firewall: Most routers will feature a built-in firewall that may be turned off and on as you require. But you need to confirm it is on, as not all manufacturers will have it turned on by default. A firewall is a filter that prevents illegal network access while letting safe network traffic through.

Turn off Remote administration: Remote administration allows you to manage or change your router settings remotely. This feature can be a wonderful addition if you have a need; However, we recommend you turn it off. Making changes remotely to your router is dangerous because if something fails, you would be locked out of the equipment. It is better to make any modifications when you are securely connected at home.

Enabling Wi-Fi Encryption

The next step to secure your Wi-Fi network is to activate encryption through your router's management console. While newer routers typically have encryption enabled by default, if you're using an older model, you'll need to enable encryption and choose a secure protocol. Here are a few encryption options you might encounter:

Wired Equivalent Privacy (WEP): This is the old guard. WEP was the pioneer in Wi-Fi encryption. It is a security protocol developed in the 1990s by the Wi-Fi Alliance. The Wi-Fi Alliance is a consortium of about 600 companies that work together on Wi-Fi-related devices and set Wi-Fi technology and security standards. WEP is like an ancient code that is not so secret anymore. It is susceptible to hacking, and security experts don't recommend using it. If your Wi-Fi system offers only WEP, it is like using an old lock that anyone with some skill can pick.

Wi-Fi Protected Access (WPA): WAP is a step up from WEP. Realizing WEP's weaknesses, WPA came along as an improved version. In 2003, it introduced more robust encryption methods, making it more challenging for unauthorized users to crack the code. It is like upgrading your lock to something sturdier. However, it is still not foolproof.

WPA2: This became the standard for many years. WPA2 was released in 2004. It is an improved version of WPA that uses even more robust encryption methods. You can think of it as the double lock system on your front door. It added an extra layer of security. WPA2 is widely used and considered secure, but like everything else, it is not invincible because it has vulnerabilities as well.

In some older routers, you may see the option to use WPA2/WPA mixed mode, which means if a device can't communicate using WPA2, it will use the lower protocol WPA. By doing so, you are forfeiting the stronger security provided by WPA2, which is not good, so we will not recommend using WPA2 in mixed mode.

WPA3: The new kid on the block, WPA3. It was released in 2018. WPA3 uses the greatest Wi-Fi encryption. It is like having a high-tech, futuristic lock on your digital door. It brings improved security features, protects against new attack methods, and enhances privacy. Devices that support the WPA3 ensure a higher level of security, especially in public Wi-Fi networks.

Choosing the right encryption is important. When picking an encryption protocol, a newer one is better. If your device and router support WPA3, that's the way to go. It provides the highest level of security.

However, if your equipment is older and doesn't support WPA3, WPA2 is still a solid choice. It is crucial to match your encryption level with the sensitivity of the data you are transmitting. If you are processing confidential information, opt for the latest and most secure encryption available.

Think of encryption as sealing an envelope. WEP is like a poorly glued envelope anyone can open. WPA is like using a sticker seal; it's better but not tamper-proof. WPA2 is like sealing with tape, and WPA3 is like using a high-tech, unbreakable seal. As technology advances, it is essential to keep your encryption methods up-to-date for a safer and more secure online experience.

Using Strong Wi-Fi Passwords

To secure your Wi-Fi network, you must create a strong and unique password. A strong password serves as the first line of defense against unauthorized access to your network and the devices connected to it. Your password should include both uppercase and lowercase letters, numbers, and special characters. This combination of characters dramatically improves the complexity of your password, making it far more difficult for potential hackers to guess or crack. Instead of selecting a simple password like *password123*, choose something more complex, such as *Tr@v3l!ng2023$*. The enhanced complexity of the password significantly minimizes the possibility of unwanted network access.

Avoid using the same password for several accounts or devices. Reusing passwords may appear easy, but it can have severe repercussions if one of your accounts is compromised. If a hacker gains access to one of your accounts and discovers that you use the same password for your Wi-Fi network, they can simply breach your home network and gain access to your connected devices, stealing sensitive information or inflicting additional damage.

It's also important not to share your Wi-Fi password with anyone, even trusted friends or family members. The more people that have access to your password, the greater the risk that it will fall into the wrong hands. If you've already given your password to someone and are concerned about the security of your network, change it right away. This proactive action will help reduce the potential security threats related to the shared password.

Changing your Wi-Fi password is a simple operation that can usually be done via your router's settings. To access these options, enter your router's web-based interface with the default login credentials provided by the router's manufacturer. Once logged in, navigate to the wireless settings section and look for the option to change your Wi-Fi password. Enter a new, strong password and save the changes. After updating your password, rejoin all of your devices to the Wi-Fi network with the new password.

Guest Network

If your Wi-Fi router supports it, make sure you enable the guest network. Newer Wi-Fi routers support guest Wi-Fi networks, allowing you to share your Internet with your guests. It will enable them to access the Internet while keeping them from accessing your primary network, where your other devices are. But if you give them access to your main network, they can see your other devices, such as printers, tablets, or smartphones.

When you enable the guest network in your router, the router creates a sub-network from your primary network. After that, it uses a firewall rule to block access from the guest network to your home network or primary network.

The guest network will have its own SSID or network name, which you can change to whatever you want. You may be tempted, however, to leave the guest network open so they don't have to ask you for a password. It wouldn't be safe, as a malicious actor in the neighborhood could connect to your network and do whatever he wants on the Internet, which could lead back to you. Also, the malicious actor can spy on your guests and steal unencrypted data sent over the guest network. Remember, we discussed sniffing attacks and man-in-the-middle attacks? So if your wireless router doesn't support the guest network, we recommend purchasing a new one.

Updating Router Firmware

In simple terms, firmware converts your usual router to a smart device and regulates your router's performance, thus keeping your network safe. As with the operating system of your PC, your router's firmware has to be updated several times for specific reasons, such as fixing bugs, adding new features, and addressing security vulnerabilities.

Unfortunately, most users don't know they need to update their firmware, a situation that may lead to a security breach. This process to access the settings to update your firmware differs from brand to brand and the model of your router. Normally, this can be accomplished by going to the router web interface. When you log in, head to the section that is dedicated to firmware or system updating, where the option to turn on automatic updates should be available. If you are not familiar with the instructions for your particular router, refer to the manual or search on the manufacturer's website for in-depth knowledge.

When settling on a new router, keep in mind to select a model from a brand that is well known in the industry for the reputation they have for security and regular firmware updates. Research reviews and features to get a router that fits your needs precisely.

Home Network Security

In this section, we'll discuss network segmentation. We'll then delve into securing IoT (Internet of Things) devices on your home network. We'll cover secure file sharing through email and conclude with strategies for network monitoring and implementing parental control measures.

Network Segmentation

Network segmentation is a strategy corporations employ to divide large networks into smaller, more manageable ones, enhancing monitoring and bolstering performance and security. So, why should you segment your home network? By segmenting your network, you can place sensitive data and devices on one network, smart home devices like thermostats on another, and even have a separate network for guests. This approach ensures that if a malicious actor gains access to your smart home network, they won't be able to reach your primary network, where your sensitive data and personal devices reside. Just as large companies utilize network segmentation to fortify their networks, you can also enhance your overall network security through segmentation.

Internet of Things (IoT) Security

Let's discuss how to secure the Internet of Things, or IoT. IoT refers to the network of everyday devices connected to the Internet that can communicate with each other. This includes smart thermostats, security cameras, smart fridges, and wearable devices like fitness trackers. The idea is to make these devices *smart* by allowing them to collect and exchange data to make our lives more convenient. Unfortunately, these devices are not secure.

Although IoT technology brings significant convenience, it also presents security challenges. Here are some reasons why IoT devices are insecure:

1. **Limited Security Measures:** Many IoT devices are designed with a focus on functionality and cost, often neglecting robust security features. This makes them vulnerable to attacks.

2. **Use of Outdated Software:** IoT manufacturers use outdated software libraries, and some IoT devices might not even receive regular software updates. As a result, hackers can exploit their vulnerabilities.

3. **Weak Passwords:** Some IoT devices come with default passwords that users cannot change. Weak or easily guessable passwords make it easier for hackers to get unauthorized access.

4. **Lack of Standardization:** The IoT landscape lacks standard-ization in terms of security protocols. Creating a unified and secure environment is challenging since each device might have different security measures. One device might use a communication protocol such as Zwave, while another might use Zigbee, Wi-Fi, and Bluetooth.

In 2016, the Mirai worm, which targeted consumer devices like smart cameras and home routers and used these devices to create an extensive network of bots, was used to launch distributed denial-of-service attacks on Amazon, Twitter, and PayPal. As a result, those websites were down for a while. In 2017, hackers exploited a computer connected to a fishing tank to hack a casino. The sensors to regulate the temperature, food, and cleanliness of the tank were connected to that computer, and hackers were able to hack the casino via the sensor. As you can see, there's a need for you to protect yourself against such attacks. But what can you do?

Here are a few things you can do to protect yourself against this threat.

1. **Change the Default Credentials:** Always change the default usernames and passwords on your IoT devices. Use a strong, unique password for each device.

2. **Regular Software Updates:** Check for firmware or software updates for your IoT devices. It ensures that you are using the most recent security patches. If you recall, we covered three important reasons you need software updates.

3. **Network Segmentation:** Segment your network and create a separate network for your IoT devices. It's like putting them in a separate room away from your critical devices, like computers and smartphones. If one IoT device is compromised, it reduces the risk to the rest of your network.

4. **Use a Strong Network Password:** Make sure your Wi-Fi network has a strong password. You could think of this as a secure lock for the front door.

5. **Implement Network Encryption:** As we previously mentioned, use WPA3 encryption for your Wi-Fi network. Encryption is like speaking a secret code that only your devices can understand. If your router is too old or you cannot use WPA3, buy a new one.

6. **Use a Firewall:** Consider having a firewall for your home network. It acts as a barrier between your devices and potential threats. Again, that can be done using your Internet router.

7. **Regularly Review Device Permissions:** Some IoT devices request access to various data. View and limit these permissions to only what is necessary. Your privacy is important.

It is like deciding which rooms your guests can enter in your home.

Buy Trusted Brands: Choose IoT devices from reputable manufacturers with a track record of providing security updates. It is like buying from a trustworthy store rather than a shady one.

By following these measures, you can create a more secure environment for your IoT devices, reducing the risk of unauthorized access and potential security breaches. As we often emphasize, just as you would secure your physical doors, it's crucial to safeguard the virtual doors of your digital home.

Secure File Sharing and Printing

How often have you emailed the wrong person? Imagine you have sent your tax return information to a stranger. Besides, the person will know about your finances, but they can steal your identity. So, securing sensitive files when you are sharing them is crucial. There are some simple steps you can follow to securely share files.

1. **Use end-to-end encryption:** With end-to-end encryption, only you and the message's recipient can read the email. However, it requires some configuration on both sides. ProtonMail, Gmail, and Outlook can send end-to-end encryption emails.

2. **File Encryption:** The second way to share sensitive information securely is by encrypting the file before attaching it to an email. You can use software like WinZip, which gives you an encryption option, or even free software like 7-zip to encrypt your files before emailing them as an attachment to the person or yourself.

3. **Use VPN:** Open Wi-Fi at coffee shops, airports, and other public places is often unsecured, so using a VPN to encrypt your Internet traffic is a good practice. The VPN creates a virtual tunnel where your data will travel, and your data is also encrypted inside the tunnel.

4. **Use Secure Printing:** If you're in the office and need to print confidential documents, utilize a secure print release system. This system works by queuing your print job; it won't automatically print. Instead, you must physically go to the printer and enter a code or use a badge to verify your identity before the job is released.

5. **Password Protect Your Folders:** if you share a computer, you can protect your files by placing them in a password- protected folder.

Network Monitoring

A network monitoring tool tracks activity on your home network. It shows you which devices are currently connected and alerts you if a new device joins. This enables you to spot unauthorized devices accessing your network. The tool can scan your entire network to detect potential security threats.

Parental Control Apps

Parental control is a feature or piece of software designed to help parents restrict and monitor their children's online activities. Let's cover why parents should use parental control apps to protect their children.

1. **Online Safety:** Parental controls help block access to age-appropriate content, ensuring children are not exposed to explicit or harmful material online.

2. **Home Network Monitoring:** It allows parents to keep an eye on their children's online activities, helping them identify and prevent potential cyberbullying situations.

3. **Time Management:** Parental controls enable parents to limit the time children spend online, promoting a healthy balance between screen time and other activities.

4. **Protection Against Online Predators:** Home Network Mon-itoring can include features allowing parents to monitor online communications, helping protect children from potential online predators.

5. **Ensuring Productivity:** To Block access to distracting websites and apps during study or bedtime hours, ensuring that children stay focused on their homework or get a good night's sleep.

6. **Device Security:** Home network monitoring can detect unusual or harmful activities on connected devices, helping protect the entire household from malware and cyber threats.

7. **Privacy Management:** Parental controls and monitoring tools provide an opportunity for parents to educate their children about online privacy, teaching them to be cautious about sharing personal information.

8. **Peace of Mind for Parents:** With home network monitor-ing, parents can remotely check on their children's online activities, providing peace of mind when not physically present.

9. **Customizing Access to Different Ages**: Parental control apps often offer settings that can be customized based on the age of each child, allowing parents to tailor access restrictions according to individual needs.

10. **Promotes Healthy Digital Habits:** Parental controls and monitoring tools serve as tools for teaching children responsible and safe Internet usage and instilling good digital habits from a young age.

Home network monitoring and parental controls are not about restricting freedom but about fostering a secure and supportive online environment. By using these tools, parents can balance allowing exploration of the digital world by ensuring children navigate it safely and responsibly.

Tips

Implementing these practical tips can significantly enhance the security posture of your home network, providing peace of mind in an increasingly interconnected digital world.

1. Update your router's firmware regularly and change the default username and password to a strong, unique combination.

2. Separate your IoT devices from your main network by creating a guest network. This minimizes potential vulnerabilities and isolates any compromised devices.

3. Set up and customize parental controls on devices used by children to limit access to inappropriate content and monitor their online activities for enhanced safety.

Recap

In this chapter, we embarked on a comprehensive exploration of how to secure home networks. We explained hardening techniques for routers, highlighting how modifying default settings and implementing strong passwords can act as an initial line of defense against unauthorized access. We emphasized the significance of network segmentation. This strategy involves dividing a large network into smaller, isolated networks to enhance monitoring and improve overall security.

The proliferation of Internet of Things (IoT) devices in households brings both convenience and potential vulnerabilities. We discussed best practices to secure these interconnected devices, ensuring they do not become entry points for cyber threats.

Secure file transfer and print practices were also spotlighted. We explored methods to safeguard confidential documents when printing, emphasizing secure print release features and password-protected folders for enhanced data protection.

Recognizing that vigilance is key, we delved into network monitoring. Implementing a network monitoring tool can provide real-time insights into connected devices and highlight any suspicious activities, allowing for timely interventions.

Lastly, we underscored the importance of parental controls in an era where digital literacy begins at a young age. Setting up robust parental controls can empower parents to manage and monitor their children's online activities, ensuring a safer browsing experience.

In Chapter 8, we'll discuss applicable strategies for personal and enterprise mobile devices. By implementing these advanced strategies, organizations can foster a culture of security awareness and mitigate potential risks associated with mobile device usage.

Chapter 8:
Enhancing Mobile Security: Advanced Strategies for Personal and Enterprise Devices

Mobile security is crucial in today's digital age, where our smartphones hold a treasure trove of personal and corporate information. We will cover some security measures an organization can implement to protect itself against data breaches. Some of these controls also apply to individuals who want to protect themselves and their families.

Understanding Mobile Security

Mobile devices such as laptops, smartphones, and tablets are susceptible to various security threats because of their portability and frequent use. Therefore, understanding mobile security involves comprehending the measures and strategies to protect mobile devices, applications, networks, and the data they handle from potential threats and vulnerabilities. It encompasses the knowledge and practices necessary to ensure information confidentiality, integrity, and availability on mobile platforms. Here are key aspects of mobile security:

1. **Threat Landscape:** Understanding the threat landscape and the various risks and threats that mobile devices face, such as

malware, phishing attacks, data breaches, and unauthor-ized access, is the starting point for a company to protect its mobile devices.

2. **Device Security:** Knowing how to configure mobile devices securely involves establishing strong passwords or biometric authentication, enabling device encryption, and keeping the device's operating system and applications up-to-date. Establishing a process or procedure for dealing with lost or stolen devices. Understanding the protocols for dealing with lost or stolen devices, including remote wipe capabilities to protect sensitive data.

3. **Network Security:** network security includes awareness of secure Wi-Fi practices, including connecting to trusted networks, using VPNs for added encryption, and avoiding public Wi-Fi for sensitive data transactions. Also, the company will need to have measures in place for its application to ensure they are transmitting data to the server over a secure connection and that the data is encrypted.

4. **App Security:** The company should know permission is requested by mobile applications, and the potential risks associated with granting excessive access to personal information can have security implications. Also, the company should know the importance of downloading apps only from official app stores to mitigate the risk of downloading malicious software.

5. **Data Protection:** Knowing the role of encryption in safeguarding data on mobile devices and ensuring that sensitive information stored on the device is encrypted to prevent unauthorized access.

6. **User Awareness:** educating users about common tactics used in phishing and social engineering attacks, emphasizing the importance of skepticism and cautious behavior to also follow security best practices, such as the importance of regular updates,

strong authentication, and reporting any suspicious activities to the IT or the security department.

7. **Mobile Device Management (MDM):** Mobile Device Management solutions help organizations manage and secure mobile devices, especially in enterprise settings, where multiple devices must be monitored and controlled.

8. **Regulatory Compliance:** A company needs to understand its legal and regulatory obligations related to mobile device security. This way, they will ensure the organization can comply with relevant laws to protect users' privacy and sensitive data.

In summary, understanding mobile security involves knowing the risk, implementing best practices, and staying informed about evolving threats in the mobile landscape. The mobile landscape is a very dynamic field with so many daily threats, so it requires ongoing education and adaptability to effectively address emerging challenges. We will cover some countermeasures a company should implement.

Mobile Device Security Strategies

Implementing a mobile device policy is essential for organizations to safeguard security, optimize efficiency, and promote responsible usage of mobile devices in the workplace. Such a policy serves as a foundational step towards enhancing organizational security. Let's delve into the key reasons highlighting the importance of having a mobile device policy.

1. **Security and Data Protection:** If not correctly managed, mobile devices can be a potential gateway for unauthorized access to sensitive company information. A mobile device policy helps establish security measures to prevent data breaches. Also, a security policy can mandate encryption and a strong authentication method, ensuring its data remains protected even if a device is lost or stolen.

2. **Network Integrity:** A policy can define guidelines for accessing the organization's network from mobile devices, ensuring that connections are secure and sensitive data is transmitted safely. Policies can also include antivirus software provisions and regular updates to protect against malware and other security threats.

3. **Employee Productivity:** Mobile device policies can set expectations for appropriate device use outside of working hours, promoting healthy work-life balance among employees. In addition, with the rise of remote work, a mobile device policy can outline protocols for accessing company resources remotely, fostering productivity while maintaining security.

4. **Device Management:** A standardized policy can establish standards for approved devices, operating systems, and applications, simplifying IT management and support. An organization can enforce policies requiring regular updates and patches to ensure that devices run the latest, most secure software.

5. **Legal and Compliance Obligations:** Many industries have specific regulations regarding protecting sensitive data, such as HIPAA, PCI, etc. A mobile device policy helps ensure the organization complies with these legal obligations. The policy can clarify the organization's stand on monitoring and accessing employees' devices or BYOD, balancing security needs with employee privacy rights.

6. **Cost Management:** Policies can address reimbursement for work-related use of personal devices, ensuring fair compensation for employees and controlling costs for the organization. Having a policy in place also aids with tracking and managing company-owned mobile devices, preventing loss and misuse.

7. **Communication and Education:** A mobile device policy is a communication tool to educate employees about the potential

risks associated with mobile device usage and the importance of responsible behavior. The policy can outline employee training and security guidelines, best practices, and proper mobile device usage.

A mobile device policy is crucial to an organization's overall cybersecurity strategy and operational efficiency. It provides a framework for managing the risks associated with mobile device usage, while promoting responsible and secure practices among employees.

A mobile device policy should also have these requirements.

- All devices must have Mobile Device Management (MDM) and Mobile Application Management (MAM).

- The type of devices that can be used.

- The minimum operating system version that the company will support.

- Whether IT can remotely lock and wipe the device.

- The minimum password requirement.

- What company data can users access on their personal devices?

Use Passwords or Biometric Authentication

The most basic measure of protecting unauthorized access to mobile devices is to make employees lock their devices either by using a strong password/PIN or biometric authentication. This one simple but effective action guarantees that the device's sensitive data continues to stay safe even when the device is lost or stolen. However, some employees prioritize convenience over security by choosing simple, easily guessed PINs like *1234* or *0000*. These weak passwords can be further compromised by criminals using techniques such as shoulder surfing or brute-force attacks.

Shoulder surfing involves observing the victim as they enter their login credentials, while brute-force attacks involve systematically trying all combinations until the correct password is found. Considering these risks, companies should strictly enforce security policies, and employees should be required to set up strong passwords or PINs that provide adequate protection for their devices.

Interestingly, biometric authentication is the alternative, which is far more efficient than passcodes for opening mobile devices. Biometric identification relies on the individual's unique biological traits, such as the fingerprint pattern, eye-iris configuration, etc., to authenticate and then provide access rights to the device.

The recent trend toward mobile device biometrics involves the use of fingerprint scanners and facial recognition software. Fingerprint scanners, the most commonly used feature in smartphones and tablets, can unlock the devices by placing one's registered finger on the scanner pad, which has been sensorized. This is commonly believed to be more secure, as fingerprints are unique to every single person and would neither be replicated nor guessed easily.

In contrast to the password mechanism, which verifies the credentials by matching them to their versions stored in the device, the facial recognition technology relies on information extracted from the facial features. This technology has become so prevalent in the past few years that most smartphones with advanced features now have facial recognition systems in order to identify users even in low-light conditions or while wearing accessories such as glasses or hats. Biometric authentication in the workplace enhances security by using unique physiological or behavioral characteristics like fingerprints or facial recognition to verify individual identities.

This method provides more reliable access control to physical and digital resources compared to traditional methods like passwords. It improves convenience and efficiency for employees by eliminating the need to manage multiple passwords or access cards, ultimately boosting productivity. Biometric systems reduce the risk of fraud, identity theft, and unauthorized access, safeguarding both employee and corporate data. Implementing biometrics can lead to cost savings by minimizing password resets, replacing lost access cards, and mitigating security incidents. It also helps organizations demonstrate compliance with regulations and internal security policies, promoting accountability among employees. Lastly, biometric authentication is adaptable to technological advancements, allowing organizations to maintain and strengthen security measures against evolving threats. Biometric data such as retina scans and fingerprints are all stored on the device itself and are not accessible to third parties, improving the security of the system altogether.

Keep Software and Apps Up-to-Date

Like with your computer, keeping your mobile operating system, apps, and security software up to date is crucial. Updates often contain patches for security vulnerabilities, so staying current is like having a shield against potential threats. Mobile device management facilitates software patching. However, for small companies without such software, enabling automatic updates on devices and prompting users to install updates when notified is crucial.

Be Cautious with App Downloads

Stick to official app stores like Google Play or Apple Store to protect yourself from downloading malicious apps. These platforms vet apps for security. Avoid downloading apps from third-party sources. Downloading apps from third-party sources is like buying goods from a street vendor. It is crucial to thoroughly review customer feedback, encompassing both five-star and one-star ratings. This is because malicious actors often purchase fake reviews, which are usually five-star ratings without substantive comment. Read the terms of service and privacy policy to know what information they'll collect about you and for what purpose.

Enable Find My Device or Remote Wipe

Mobile devices can easily be lost or stolen. Android and iOS offer services like *Find My Phone* that help you locate, lock, or erase your device if it is lost or stolen. It's like having a GPS tracker for your digital companion. To prevent company data from being leaked, enabling remote wipe is important. The feature allows an administrator to send a command to delete the data on the phone remotely if the phone has power and access to the Internet. The bad actors have gotten so smart by preventing the stolen phone from connecting to the Internet so it doesn't get located or wiped out.

Another way to erase the data on the phone is by contacting the carrier. They will issue a remote wipe command to the device if it has phone signals.

Avoid Public Wi-Fi for Sensitive Activities

Public Wi-Fi networks are often unsecured, making them vulnerable to eavesdropping or man-in-the-middle attacks, which can lead to the data being compromised. Avoid using public Wi-Fi for sensitive transactions. If you must connect to public networks, consider using a virtual private network, or VPN, which we will discuss in the next section. A VPN is like adding an extra protection layer when using public spaces. If you don't have a VPN, it is better to use the hotspot on your phone, as it is a private Internet connection that you control.

Use a Virtual Private Network (VPN)

When connecting to public Wi-Fi, it is vital to use a reputable VPN service to encrypt your Internet traffic and protect your data from potential snooping. Imagine you are sending a letter, but instead of sending it directly from your house to your friend's house, you decide to send it through a secret tunnel. That tunnel is your VPN, so let's explain how it works.

What is the core functionality of a VPN?

1. **Establishing a Connection:** When you connect to a VPN, your device, like your computer or smartphone, creates a secure, encrypted connection to a server owned by the VPN provider. It is like having a secret meeting point before sending your letter.

2. **Encryption Phase:** Which is the secret sauce of VPNs? Your data is encrypted, so it becomes a secret code only you, your friend, or the intended recipient can understand.

3. **Browsing Through the Tunnel:** Once your connection is established and your data is encrypted, it travels through the

virtual tunnel created by the VPN. It is like a letter going through an underground passage, safe from prying eyes.

4. **IP Address Masking:** Your device has a unique identifier called an IP address. An IP address is like the return address on your letter. With a VPN, your IP address gets replaced with the address of the VPN server. It's like sending your letter from the secret meeting point instead of your home.

5. **Accessing Restricted Content:** Because your IP address is now that of the VPN server, it can appear like you are accessing the Internet from a different location. It's like a letter; even though it was sent from your secret meeting point, it appears it came from a different town. It allows you to access restricted content from your location.

6. **Security on Public Networks:** When you use public Wi-Fi, like in a coffee shop or at the airport, it's like sending your letter from a crowded street. It's more susceptible to prying eyes. A VPN adds an extra layer of security, making it more like sending your letter from a private, secure room, even if you are in a crowded place.

7. **Privacy and anonymity:** A VPN provides higher privacy by masking your IP address and encrypting your data. It is like sending an anonymous letter without revealing your address or the content.

A VPN is like a secure secret tunnel for your Internet connection. It encrypts your data, hides your IP address, and allows you to access the Internet more privately and securely. Whether you want to protect your data on public Wi-Fi, access region-restricted content, or enhance your online privacy, a VPN is a handy tool in your digital toolbox.

Types of VPNS

Virtual private networks (VPNs) can be categorized based on their functionality, architecture, and the protocol they use. Here are the main VPNs.

1. **Remote Access VPN, also known as Client-to-Server VPN:** Remote Access VPN is the one that you are most familiar with. If you work remotely for a company with VPN access, they will install a client or a server on your company's laptop to allow you to VPN in. This type of VPN is like a secure tunnel between you and your company's network. It is used by individuals who work remotely for a company and need access to its data.

2. **SSL VPN:** Not all employees have a company laptop to work from home. The company will allow these users to use their personal computers to connect to the company's network. The users will enter the login credentials at a specific web browser address. It will initiate a secure connection for them to connect to the company's network. Once the secure connection is established, the user can access the office computer, specific applications, or private network services defined by the company.

3. **Site-to-site VPN:** This type of VPN is mainly used by large companies with multiple locations. This VPN connects the entire network rather than individual devices. The data flows securely between these locations as if they were all part of the same local network.

When utilizing a VPN service from providers such as NordVPN or ExpressVPN, the service provider manages the servers. However, organizations typically manage their VPN servers.

Each type of VPN has its own set of advantages and is suitable for specific use cases. The choice of VPN type depends on the organization's requirements, the nature of the data being transmitted, and the level of security needed.

Backup Your Data regularly

Imagine your phone as a digital diary, storing cherished memories, important contacts, and vital information you rely on daily. It's your trusted companion, holding photos of special moments with loved ones and messages that mark significant events. Losing the data on your phone would be devastating, so it's crucial to regularly back up your mobile device as part of your personal cybersecurity routine.

To ensure the saving of your digital diary and the safekeeping of your special memories and important information, you have to periodically backup the data stored on your phone. Generating your backup means you have to create a copy of all the crucial items on the device, like documents, photos, videos, contacts, and important files on the device, and then keep it in a safe and separate location. With this approach, you can always have peace of mind, knowing that if something happens to your mobile phone, all your data remains secure and accessible.

There are several ways to back up your mobile device's data, each with its own advantages:

- **Cloud Backup:** Utilizing an online cloud service is a fast and common method to save data from your phone. Cloud backup technology allows your data to be transmitted to a remote server accessible anywhere with an internet connection. Major smartphone manufacturers like Apple and Google offer built-in cloud storage services (iCloud & G-Drive) that automatically sync your data to their servers. Third-party services like Dropbox or OneDrive offer similar cloud backup capabilities.

- **External Device Backup:** Besides cloud backups, you can also use another device, like a computer or external hard disk, to back up your phone's data. This method involves connecting your phone to the external device and transferring data through physical means, such as a USB cable, Wi-Fi, or Bluetooth. Once the transfer is complete, you can disconnect your phone and securely store the external device. A significant advantage of this method is that you can access and manage your data without an internet connection, as it is stored on your local media. While it may require more manual effort, some may find it preferable to cloud backup.

- **Hybrid Backup:** This method combines the advantages of both cloud services and external storage devices like hard disks. With this approach, your phone's data is continuously backed up to an external device. You upload these backups to a cloud service, providing maximum data protection. Having two copies of your data—one locally and one in the cloud—increases security. In the event of a backup failure or inaccessible media, you still have the alternative copy, ensuring you don't lose your important data.

Tips

Here are some tips to secure your home network and mobile devices:

1. Be smart about smart home technology by using secure settings.

2. Enable automatic updates for your device's operating system and apps to ensure you have the latest security patches. Regularly check for updates if automatic updates are not an option for the device or software.

3. Only download apps from official app stores like Google Play Store or Apple App Store to minimize the risk of malware. Before downloading an app, read user reviews and ratings to gauge its reliability and security.

Recap

We discussed critical mobile security practices, including the necessity of setting a passcode to safeguard phone access and consistently updating phone operating systems and applications. For businesses, the utilization of Mobile Device Management (MDM) software was emphasized.

We elaborated on the risks associated with downloading apps, even from reputable sources like the App Store. We cautioned against transmitting sensitive information over public Wi-Fi networks and highlighted the role of VPNs in safeguarding privacy.

Therefore, the following chapter will discuss corporate network tools and technologies for security. We will explore firewalls, intrusion detection, and prevention systems, security information, and event management solutions, end-point protection platforms, access control systems, reasons for having your solutions regularly audited, and penetration testing done.

In Chapter 9, we'll cover important cybersecurity tools and technologies designed to protect network infrastructure against cyberattacks and unauthorized access.

Chapter 9:
Cybersecurity Tools and Technologies

We now move on to Chapter 9, examining cybersecurity tools and technologies. Here in this chapter, we will focus our attention on five key areas. To commence, we will delve into the network security tools corporations utilize to fortify organizational defenses. We will delve into the intricate world of virtual private networks (VPNs) and the diverse array of VPN options available, providing a comprehensive overview.

Following that, we will shed light on the concept of encryption and the myriad types prevalent in today's market. We will delve into the intricacies of securing messages, exploring various solutions and techniques for safeguarding communications. Lastly, we will delve into the concept of defense in depth, elucidating its significance and the imperative for organizations to adopt this strategic approach in fortifying their defenses against cyber threats.

Network Security Tools

We will have a closer look at cybersecurity devices and technologies designed to safeguard a firm from cyberthreats. We will investigate firewalls, IDS, IPS, SIEMS, vulnerability scanners, and cloud security monitoring tools. These technologies are vital for identifying, detecting, and preventing threats from hackers.

Firewalls

A firewall is a security device or a program that monitors network traffic and detects potential threats. The primary purpose of a firewall is to act as a barrier that will block any malicious traffic and allow non-malicious traffic to get inside the network.

From a network security perspective, firewalls and routers are considered gatekeepers, ensuring only good information gets in and out. The traffic is handled based on predetermined security rules.

There are several types of firewalls and understanding them requires distinguishing between their placement or where they function within the network and their operational technology or the methods they employ.

Network-Based Firewall: Network- based firewalls protect the entire network or segment by filtering traffic at the network edge.

Host-based firewall: A host-based firewall is software installed on a computer or a server to monitor the traffic on the device. A host-based firewall effectively protects against threats that may originate from the device itself.

Web Application Firewall: The web application firewall helps to protect web applications by filtering and monitoring HTTP traffic between the application and the Internet. A web application firewall is also called a WAF. The Web Application Firewall protects against common web-based threats, including SQL injection and cross-site scripting.

Cloud-Based Firewall: A cloud-based firewall protects data, applications, and infrastructure hosted in the cloud. It is ideal for organizations leveraging cloud services for data storage, computing power, and application hosting.

The second type of firewall is classified by how it operates.

Packet Filtering Firewall

Before going any further, let's explain what a network packet is. A network packet is like a small parcel of information that travels across a network from one place to another. Imagine you're sending a letter through the mail. The letter contains your message, and you put it in an envelope with an address on it.

Similarly, a network packet contains data, such as a piece of a webpage or an email, and it has an address called an IP address that tells it where to go. Along the way, routers and switches help the packet find its destination by reading the address and passing it along until it reaches its final destination. Once it arrives, the recipient's computer opens the packet and reads the data inside, just like opening an envelope to read a letter.

Packet-filtering firewalls examine packets of data as they pass through the network. They allow or block packets based on predefined rules, such as source and destination IP addresses, protocols, and port numbers. This type of firewall is simple and efficient for basic traffic filtering. However, they are limited in terms of complex filtering and may not inspect the content of packets, meaning they may let malicious traffic from bad actors get inside your network.

Stateful Firewalls: These firewalls look at individual packets and keep track of the state of active connections. They make decisions based on the context of the traffic, allowing or blocking it based on the state of the connection. Stateful firewalls offer improved security by considering the context of the network connections. However, they can be very resource-intensive and may not provide the deep packet inspection needed to protect your network.

Next-Generation Firewalls: Next-generation firewalls come with traditional features and advanced security technologies, including Intrusion Prevention Systems (IPS), deep packet inspection, and application awareness. The aim is to provide a comprehensive security solution. This type of firewall is suitable for advanced threat detection and prevention capabilities. However, they are very complex to configure and may require regular updates to stay effective against evolving threats.

For a company to benefit from the protection provided by firewalls, it is crucial not only to choose the correct firewalls but also to configure them properly.

Routers

The router is a network device that guides and directs traffic between networks, subnetworks, and devices on the network by forwarding packets to the intended IP addresses. It also allows multiple devices, like your home router, to use the same Internet. A router often has a built-in firewall that checks incoming and outgoing traffic, ensuring nothing harmful gets in. Your home router, for example, will assign a unique local address to each device at home. When these devices talk to the Internet, it translates the local addresses into a single public address to protect the devices on your home network against direct attacks from the Internet.

Intrusion Detection Systems (IDS) and Intrusion Prevention Systems (IPS)

An Intrusion Detection System is a security tool that can be an appliance or software placed behind a firewall. It monitors inbound and outbound traffic for any signs of malicious activity. It analyzes the network activity to learn what normal behavior looks like and raises the alarm if it spots anything unusual for the network administrator to investigate.

Like firewalls, there are different types of IDS.

Network-Based IDS (NIDS): They are deployed strategically to monitor incoming and outgoing traffic.

Host-Based IDS (HIDS): HIDS is installed on a specific server or endpoint to monitor traffic coming in and out of that server or endpoint.

Signature-based IDS: Signature-based IDS monitors the entire network traffic and compares it with a database of known threats. Even though IDS can detect malicious activity, it doesn't take action. Intrusion Prevention Systems will take action, like resetting the connection, blocking the source IP address, or dropping the network packets when they see something suspicious.

IPSs are similar to intrusion detection systems because they are also placed behind the firewall; the only difference is that you must place them between the source and the destination traffic. IPS can actively block or prevent certain types of traffic it identifies as harmful.

There are several types of IPSs.

Network-Based IPS: This system operates at the network level, monitoring the traffic that flows through a network. It can detect and prevent malicious activities based on predefined signatures or anomalies in the network traffic. This type of IPS is effective at identifying and blocking threats before they reach individual devices within the network.

Host-based IPS: Unlike network-based IPS, host-based IPS monitors an individual device, such as a server or workstation. It monitors the activities and behaviors of these devices, looking for signs of malicious activity or unauthorized access. This type of IPS provides an additional layer of security by focusing on the integrity of individual devices.

Network Behavior Analysis: This approach involves analyzing the patterns and behaviors of network traffic to detect abnormal or suspicious activities. Instead of relying solely on predefined signatures, network behavior analysis looks for deviations from normal network behavior. This can be useful in detecting new or unknown threats, including zero-day vulnerabilities, which may not have known signatures or patterns.

Wireless Intrusion Prevention System: A Wireless Intrusion Prevention System will scan the Wi-Fi network to identify unauthorized access and remove unauthorized devices from the network.

Security Information and Event Management (SIEM)

A SIEM is a software solution that aggregates and analyzes activity from many resources across your entire network. Here is a step-by-step explanation of how it works.

First, it collects logs from various sources within the network from devices such as servers, domain controllers, and endpoints. Because these logs come in different formats, the SIEM will normalize them in a specific format to make them uniform and understandable.

Next, it will connect the dots by correlating different events to identify patterns and potential security threats. When it detects something fishy, it will raise the alarms and notify the security team. It is also used for incident response and threat hunting because it provides insights and tools for the security team to take the necessary action.

SIEM helps organizations comply with industry regulations like PCI and log management, as it maintains detailed logs for security events. SIEM is crucial for an organization as it provides early threat detection capability and a holistic view of the security landscape, allowing organizations to understand vulnerabilities and take proactive measures.

Vulnerability Scanners

Vulnerability scanners are automated tools that allow organizations to identify and assess vulnerabilities in the computer systems, networks, and applications that bad actors could use to breach the organization. Vulnerability scanners rely on a database that contains information about known vulnerabilities. An organization can conduct different vulnerability scans.

Network Vulnerability Scanning: This scan involves identifying vulnerabilities within an organization's network infrastructure, including firewalls, routers, servers, and other network devices. By conducting scans on both the external and internal networks, the organization can pinpoint potential vulnerabilities that external threat actors may exploit to gain unauthorized access. Internal network scans are crucial for detecting insider threats.

Web Application Scanning: Web application scanning is an essential step in the cybersecurity process. This scan is designed to meticulously identify and scrutinize security vulnerabilities within web applications and websites, ensuring comprehensive protection against potential threats and cyberattacks.

Scanning Techniques

There are various techniques available for conducting scans, including authenticated and unauthenticated methods.

Authenticated or Credential Scan: This technique provides the security scanner with a valid credential, such as a username and password. These credentials grant the scanner access to the internal working network of the target system. Credential scans have a higher access level because they simulate an authorized user interacting with the system. It allows the scanner to access more detailed information about the system's configuration, installed software, and user privileges. Credential scans are often used in internal network assessments.

Unauthenticated Scans: Unauthenticated scans do not use specific credentials. They operate externally on the target system and attempt to identify vulnerabilities from the perspective of an external attacker. Unauthenticated scans have limited access and rely on available public information. They focus on identifying vulnerabilities that can be detected with no internal system access. This type of scan is quicker to perform.

Cloud Security Monitoring Tools

Cloud security monitoring tools help organizations ensure the security, compliance, and performance of their cloud infrastructure and services. As businesses increasingly adopt cloud computing, it becomes crucial to have robust monitoring tools in response to security events and potential threats in the cloud environment. These tools provide real-time visibility detection and response capabilities, contributing to a proactive and effective cloud security strategy.

Here are some key features of cloud security:

1. Logging and Event Monitoring: Cloud security monitor-ing tools collect and analyze logs and events from various cloud services and resources. They provide insights into user activities and system events that change within the cloud environment.

2. Vulnerability Detection: These tools help identify vulner-abilities and misconfigurations in cloud infrastructure and promptly address potential security gaps.

3. Threat Detection and Intelligence: Cloud security mon-itoring tools use threat intelligence and behavioral analysis to detect patterns and malicious activity. They can identify abnormal behavior, unauthorized access, or other signs of security incidents.

4. Identity and Access Monitoring: Monitoring tools track user activities and access management permissions, ensuring only authorized users have appropriate access to resources. They help detect and prevent unauthorized access or changes to users' permissions.

5. Data Protection and Encryption Monitoring: These tools monitor data stored in the cloud, ensuring that sensitive information is encrypted and protected. They can identify anomalies in data access patterns and alert administrators to potential data breaches.

6. Configuration Management: Cloud security monitoring tools ensure compliance with best practices and configuration baselines. They alert administrators to any deviation from secure configurations.

7. Incident Response and Automation: These tools help or-chestrate and automate incident response processes when a security incident occurs. They enable quick and efficient responses to security events, reducing the impact of potential breaches.

8. Compliance Monitoring: Cloud security tools ensure that cloud environments are ideal for industry-specific regulations and compliance standards. They generate reports and alerts to help organizations demonstrate their adherence to regulatory requirements.

9. **SIEM Integration**: Many cloud security monitoring tools integrate with SIEM systems to provide a centralized view of security events across both on-premises and cloud environments.

10. **Behavior Analytics:** These tools may incorporate user behavior analytics to detect abnormal patterns or user activities, helping to identify potential insider threats or compromised accounts.

11. **Continuous Monitoring:** Cloud security monitoring is a continuous process. These tools operate in real-time, ensuring that security events and potential threats are identified promptly.

Encryption

Let's talk about an important security technique employed to safeguard the confidentiality and integrity of data: encryption. We will examine the intricacies of encryption, explaining its mechanisms and exploring the various encryptions available to us. We will discuss key management best practices to ensure the effective and secure implementation of encryption methods.

Mechanism of Encryption

Imagine you are sending a letter and want to ensure no one except the intended recipient can read it. Encryption scrambles the letter's contents so that only someone with the correct key can unscramble and read it. There are four components to an encryption system.

The first one is plaintext. Plaintext is the original message, the readable message.

The second one is the scrambled data, which is called ciphertext. This is the message you get after it has been encrypted.

The third is the encryption algorithm. An encryption algorithm is like a complex set of instructions that dictates how plaintext is transformed into ciphertext. It is the secret recipe for scrambling the data.

Fourth, you have the key to unscramble the message. The key is like a special code to unlock the secret message.

Why is it worth embracing encryption despite its potential inconveniences? Encryption matters for several reasons.

1. **Data Privacy:** Encryption protects your personal and sensi-tive information, ensuring it remains private, especially during transmission or storage.

2. **Secure Communication**: Encryption helps secure commun-ication for online transactions or any network communication. Encryption ensures that the data exchange is secure and cannot be easily intercepted.

3. **Protection Against Unauthorized Access:** Encrypting stored data on devices or servers protects it from being accessed by unauthorized individuals, even if the physical device is compromised. Integrity verification hash functions help verify the integrity of data. If the hash changes, the data has been tampered with.

4. **To Build Trust:** Knowing that encryption is in place builds trust in online services and transactions, encouraging users to engage in digital activities without fear of data compromise.

Encryption Types

There are several encryption methods available that you need to be aware of, and we are going to discuss four of them.

Symmetric Encryption: With symmetric encryption, the sender and the recipient use the same key to encrypt and decrypt the message. It is fast and efficient. However, sharing the key needs to be done securely. Otherwise, if intercepted, it could compromise the message.

Asymmetric Encryption: Asymmetric encryption employs a distinct public key for encryption and a corresponding private key for decryption. The keys are mathematically related but cannot be derived from one another. The advantage of Asymmetric encryption means that it secures communication without exchanging a secret key. It is computationally more intensive than symmetric encryption.

Hash Functions: Hash functions take data and create a fixed-size string of characters called a hash. It is a one-way process. It is easy to generate the hash, but extremely difficult to reverse it to get the original data. Hash functions are often used to verify data integrity. If the data changes, the hash will also change.

Transport Layer Security (TLS) and Secure Sockets Layer (SSL): These security protocols use symmetric and asymmetric encryption to secure communication over the Internet. They ensure that your connection to a website is private and secure.

Public Key Infrastructure (PKI)

PKI is a system designed to enable two parties to confirm each other's identities and set up a secure, encrypted connection. It operates on a two-key system, utilizing the asymmetric key encryption we previously talked about, which involves both public and private keys. You might wonder how the system ensures the public key's owner is legitimate. This question leads us to explore the three main components of PKI, shedding light on its functioning.

The Certificate Authority (CA): The CA is like a trusted authority in PKI. The CA issues digital certificates that also vouch for the authenticity of a user, the device, or the service. It's similar to getting an official ID card from a government agency.

The Registration Authority (RA) verifies individuals' or entities' identities before receiving a digital certificate. It is like the application processor ensuring you meet specific criteria before getting an official ID.

The Certificate Revocation List (CRL): The CRL is like a blacklist. If a digital certificate is compromised or invalid, it is added to the CRL. The CA stores, signs, and revokes digital certificates.

PKI, or Public Key Infrastructure, is a crucial framework for ensuring secure communication over digital networks. Here are some use cases and reasons highlighting its importance:

1. **Secure Online Transactions:** PKI is widely used on e-commerce platforms to secure online transactions. When you make a purchase online and see the "https" in the address bar, it indicates that PKI is in use, encrypting the data transferred between your browser and the server.

2. **Digital Signatures:** PKI enables the creation and verification of digital signatures. This ensures the authenticity of digital documents and messages. For instance, in legal, financial, or

governmental sectors where document integrity is paramount, PKI helps in confirming the document's origin and ensuring it hasn't been tampered with.

3. **Remote Access and VPNs:** Many organizations use PKI to establish secure connections for remote access to their networks or when setting up virtual private networks (VPNs). This ensures that data exchanged between the remote user and the corporate network remains confidential and integral.

4. **Smart cards and authentication devices:** PKI is used in smart cards and authentication devices for secure physical and logical access control.

Encryption Key Management

An organization must properly manage its encryption keys to prevent its data from being compromised, even if it is encrypted. The more data the organization acquires, the more encryption key pairs it must manage.

Key management encompasses the processes of generating, distributing, storing, using, and securely disposing of cryptographic keys once they're no longer required.

Key Generation: When creating keys, a company must employ a secure key generation process to ensure optimal key strength. The strength of a key is determined by two primary factors: the randomness of the key and its length or size. Similar to crafting a strong password, a strong key serves as a formidable barrier against unauthorized access attempts by malicious actors. Therefore, when generating keys, companies can utilize a key generator.

Key Distribution: After the keys have been created, they will need to be distributed or shared with employees, partners, and applications which need to encrypt the data. To do so, a company can use software called a secret manager. They can also use the Public Key

Infrastructure (PKI) to share the public keys with anyone who needs them.

Key Storage: To prevent the keys from falling into the wrong hands, you must store them safely. You can use the Hardware Security Module (HSM) or software like Azure Vault. You must have multiple copies of your keys as backups to ensure that you can still access the data if one copy gets lost or becomes unusable. Also, keys should not be accessible to everyone. That is why you need strong access control to only grant access to a limited number of users to prevent compromise.

Key Usage: The primary objective of key usage is to enable secure cryptographic operations, including encryption to protect data confidentiality, decryption to access encrypted data, or authentication to verify the identity of users or systems.

Key Rotation: Just like passwords, it is recommended to rotate your encryption keys to limit the damage if a key is stolen, for example. Also, using the same key for a long time increases the chances that it will be compromised, so you need to rotate it at a regular interval.

Key Destruction: The company should have the ability to revoke and destroy the keys, and they need to destroy all copies of the keys at the end of the life cycle. By following these best practices, proper key management will ensure that encryption keys remain confidential and are accessible only to authorized parties.

Every organization should adhere to specific best practices to safeguard these keys against unauthorized access, preserve their integrity and confidentiality, and uphold the security of their cryptographic systems.

Secure Messaging and Email Encryption

In this last section, we will explore the realm of secure messaging within the corporate environment, utilizing secure messaging platforms and email encryption. Encryption plays a pivotal role, particularly in today's digital era, where communication frequently entails sharing sensitive and confidential data. Ensuring the security of messages and email correspondence is essential for safeguarding sensitive information's confidentiality, privacy, and integrity against potential threats such as eavesdropping, unauthorized access, or man-in-the-middle attacks.

Numerous techniques are employed within the corporate landscape to ensure the security of messages. Below, we highlight some of the most prevalent and effective methods utilized for this purpose.

End-to-End Encryption

End-to-end encryption is a secure measure that plays a crucial role in ensuring the privacy and integrity of email communication. It is a powerful encryption method that protects the content of the message from being accessed by unauthorized parties, even if the communication travels through compromised channels. End-to-end encryption is essential for several reasons.

1. **To Protect Privacy:** Encryption ensures that only the intended recipient can decrypt and read the content of an email. Even if the email passes through email servers or other intermediaries, the information remains confidential and is inaccessible to unauthorized entities.

2. **Data Integrity:** It protects against unauthorized mod-ification or tampering with the content during transit, guaranteeing that the recipient receives the message as intended.

3. **Preventing Eavesdropping and Man-in-the-Middle Attacks:** Without end-to-end encryption, emails can be intercepted and

read by unauthorized individuals during transmission. End-to-end encryption encrypts the content so that even if intercepted, it remains unreadable without the proper decryption key.

4. **Compliance**: Many privacy regulations and standards, such as GDPR, require the protection of personal data. End-to-end encryption is crucial for emails containing sensitive information, such as financial data, personal details, or business plans. It ensures that this information is not exposed to unauthorized parties during the transmission.

Pretty Good Privacy (PGP)

A second tool to protect your email communications and files is PGP. PGP is a popular data encryption and decryption program that provides cryptographic privacy and data authentication for data communications. It was created by Phil Zimmerman in 1991 and has since become a widely used method for securing emails, files, and other forms of electronic communication.

Some Components of PGP

PGP uses a combination of symmetric key cryptography and public key cryptography. Each user has a pair of keys: a public key that is shared with others and a private key that is kept secret. Data encrypted with the public key can only be decrypted by the corresponding private key. PGP allows you to do digital signatures. PGP will enable users to sign messages or files with the private key. A digital signature can attest that you are the sender of the message. The other party will verify the digital signature by using your public key. Digital signatures ensure the authenticity and integrity of the message or the file. PGP employs a decentralized trust model known as a web of trust. Instead of relying on a central authority to verify the authenticity of public keys, users can sign each other's public keys. This creates a network of trust where the validity of a public key is based on the trustworthiness of those who have signed it.

SMIME

Secure Multipurpose Internet Mail Extensions (SMIME) is a standard for securing email messages using public key cryptography. It provides a framework for encrypting and digitally signing email content, ensuring electronic communications, confidentiality, integrity, and authenticity.

SMIME is widely used for securing email communication in both personal and business settings. One of the primary purposes of SMIME is to encrypt the content of email messages. Users who want to send an encrypted email use the recipient's public key to encrypt the message. This way, only the recipient with the corresponding private key can decrypt and read the content.

SMIME uses a combination of public-key and symmetric-key cryptography. Each user has a pair of public and private keys. The public key is shared with others, while the private key is kept confidential. SMIME can sign email messages digitally. The senders will use the private key to create a digital signature, providing proof of the message's origin and ensuring its integrity. The recipients can verify the signature using the sender's public key. Companies are using SMIME as a protection against phishing attacks.

Secure File Transfer

Secure file transfers in the corporate world are critical to protect sensitive information and maintain data confidentiality, integrity, and availability. Here are some best practices for securely transferring files in the corporate environment.

The first is to use protocols like SFTP, Secure File Transfer Protocol, and HTTPS Hypertext Transfer Protocol Secure and Secure Shell File

Transfer Protocol SCP that can provide encryption during data transmission, safeguarding files from interception. Businesses can leverage VPNs for encryption and implement end-to-end encryption for file transfers. Adherence to the company's data classification guidelines is paramount. Ensuring strict compliance with data classification policies and implementing robust security measures is imperative. By doing so, highly sensitive files receive additional protection throughout the transfer process.

Tips

Here are some immediate tips to safeguard your sensitive information and privacy, particularly when utilizing public networks or Wi-Fi.

1. Consider investing in a VPN service to encrypt your communications effectively.

2. When sharing sensitive files like tax returns, utilize free encryption software options such as PGP and 7-Zip, or opt for a commercial version like WinZip to provide robust protection for your data.

Recap

In this chapter, we explored essential cybersecurity tools and technologies. We discussed the primary defense mechanisms of networks, including firewalls and routers.

We examined the utilization of IDS, IPS, and cloud security monitoring for detecting and responding to fraudulent threats. Following this, we discussed the significance of virtual private networks (VPNs) and elucidated various encryption techniques, such as asymmetric, symmetric, and TLS encryption, for securing communications. We emphasized the importance of key management in maintaining robust security measures. We explored using end-to-end SMIME and PGP encryption technologies for message protection.

In Chapter 10, we'll delve into the Defense in Depth strategy, its pivotal components, and practical insights on implementing this strategy effectively.

Chapter 10:
Defense-in-Depth Strategy

This Chapter will explore the concept of Defense in Depth, a comprehensive cybersecurity strategy that employs multiple layers of security measures to protect an organization's information systems. The idea is to create a robust and resilient security posture. By using diverse security mechanisms, this approach acknowledges that no single security measure is foolproof, and a combination of measures helps mitigate the risk of various types of cyber threats.

Understanding Defense in Depth

Organizations daily deal with cyber attackers who want to breach their systems. They must use a layered defense-in-depth strategy to defend themselves. The intent is to provide redundancy in case of a security control failure. This approach offers better threat mitigation and reduces the likelihood of a successful attack.

Layers of Defense in Depth

Here are some of the most common security elements in the Defense in Depth strategy: network security, endpoint security, application security, data security, and end-user education. Each layer addresses specific security aspects and creates a comprehensive approach.

Network Security

There are three layers a company can implement to secure its network. The first layer involves installing firewalls, followed by intrusion detection and prevention systems (IDS/IPS), and the last one is network segmentation.

Firewalls: The first line of defense when securing a network is to deploy firewalls at various entry points, like between internal networks and the Internet. These firewalls analyze all traffic to identify and block potential threats to the organization. Organizations may use either hardware or software firewalls, or sometimes both, for enhanced protection.

Intrusion Detection and Intrusion Prevention Systems: IDS monitors network or system activities for malicious or suspicious behavior. IPS takes action to block or prevent identified threats. As explained earlier, these systems are strategically placed within the network to analyze traffic patterns and detect anomalies or known attack signatures. They can operate at various levels, including the network and application layers. When operating at the network layer, IDS/IPS focus on monitoring traffic based on IP addresses, source, and destination ports, and other network-level information. At the application layer, they inspect the content of data packets, understand application-specific commands, and detect anomalies or malicious activities within specific applications. This dual-layered approach allows IDS and IPS to provide comprehensive security coverage across various stages of network communication.

Network Segmentation: The segmentation of networks is a method that has the objective of dividing a large network into several smaller, disconnected networks, or subnets. The purpose of network segmentation is to minimize the potential damage and spread of the cyberattack by controlling the communication types and access points between the different parts of the network.

Organizations can prevent total network compromise by creating distinct network segments for different divisions, internal functions, or security tiers. They can effectively mitigate threats by implementing detailed access controls and preventing unauthorized movement within the network. For instance, a company might segregate its financial, human resources, and production systems, each with its own set of policies and access restrictions.

Firewalls and Access Control Lists (ACLs) are used to separate and restrict traffic flow between network segments. This allows organizations to apply the principle of least privilege, granting users or systems only the permissions for their tasks, thus reducing the potential damage from a single breach.

Network segmentation also helps contain the spread of malware and mitigates the impact of internal attacks. If an attacker breaches one network segment, he won't be able to gain access to other parts of the network containing critical assets.

Endpoint Security

Endpoint security involves protecting individual devices, such as computers and mobile devices. For these layers, anti-malware software and endpoint detection and response are necessary to protect the organization against malicious software that can enter and spread throughout the network.

Antivirus Software: The role of antivirus software is to detect and remove malicious software or malware from individual devices, such as computers, laptops, servers, etcetera. It will continuously scan for known malware signatures or suspicious behavior. Regular updates are crucial to combating emerging threats.

Endpoint Detection and Response (EDR): EDR solutions go beyond traditional antivirus by monitoring activities on endpoints in real-time. It continuously monitors, detects, and responds to advanced threats and unusual behaviors, helping to prevent and mitigate security incidents.

Application Security

Application security is another focus layer for Defense in Depth because malicious actors can exploit vulnerabilities in software and applications. Application security involves implementing measures to protect software applications from security threats and vulnerabilities. It is a critical aspect of the overall cybersecurity strategy, as applications often serve as entry points for attackers. Some key components of application security defense in depth include:

Secure Coding Practices: The company must ensure software developers follow secure coding practices to minimize vulnerabilities from the outset. The developers will receive instruction on secure coding principles, along with best practices and guidelines for ensuring security in their code.

Code reviews: The application source code must be regularly analyzed to identify and rectify security issues. This can be done manually or with the help of automated tools to ensure that the application code is secure and free from common vulnerabilities.

Penetration Testing: Simulated cyberattacks to identify application vulnerabilities and weaknesses are essential. The company will need to regularly conduct penetration testing, where ethical hackers attempt to exploit vulnerabilities in the application. These findings will help developers and security teams address and fix identified issues.

Web Application Firewalls (WAF): A WAF provides a protective barrier between web applications and the Internet to filter and monitor HTTP traffic. The WAF will analyze and filter incoming traffic to the web applications to detect and block common web applications.

Data Security

Data security plays a central and critical role in the Defense in Depth strategy. The overarching goal of Defense in Depth is to create a multi-layered security infrastructure that safeguards an organization's assets from various cyber threats. Data is one of the most valuable assets, but it requires specialized attention and protection. Data security contributes to the Defense in Depth strategy.

Confidentiality: Data security ensures that sensitive and confidential information remains confidential and is only accessible to authorized individuals or systems. Therefore, the company must encrypt data at rest, in transit, and during processing to help maintain confidentiality. Access controls and authentication mechanisms will restrict access to data based on the user's roles and permissions.

Integrity: Data integrity ensures that information remains accurate and unaltered throughout its life cycle. The company will need to implement hash functions, checksums, and digital signatures to verify the integrity of the data. Regular integrity checks will help detect and address any unauthorized changes or corruption in the data.

Availability: Data security contributes to information availability, ensuring authorized users can access data when needed. The company will also implement redundancy measures, backups, and disaster recovery plans to maintain data availability. These measures prevent data loss and ensure business continuity during a security incident.

Prevention of Unauthorized Access: One of the primary objectives of data security is to prevent unauthorized access to sensitive information. That is why access control, strong authentication mechanisms, and least-privileged principles will help limit access to data. Again, regular audits and monitoring activities will help detect and respond to unauthorized access attempts.

Data Classification: Data security involves classifying data based on its sensitivity and importance to the organization. Classifying data helps prioritize security measures. Highly sensitive information receives enhanced protection, while less critical data may have less stringent security controls.

Data Destruction: That means safely disposing of data that is no longer needed or has reached its life cycle. Secure data disposal practices include permanently deleting or wiping data from storage devices before disposal. This prevents sensitive information from being retrieved by unauthorized individuals.

User Education

In the security world, we have the expression: *your security is as strong as the weakest link, and humans are the weakest link.* That is why educating your users about potential security threats, phishing attacks, social engineering attacks, and best security practices that can significantly reduce the risk of human errors leading to a security incident is crucial. The company needs to conduct regular security awareness training sessions for employees. Those sessions should cover identifying phishing emails, using strong passwords and reporting suspicious activities. Simulated phishing exercises can also be helpful to test and reinforce learning. The company should have a procedure to update users on emerging threats and security measures.

Defense in Depth Benefits

Defense in Depth is a comprehensive approach to cybersecurity that involves implementing multiple layers of security controls to protect an organization's assets and data. This strategy offers several key benefits that help organizations strengthen their overall security posture and minimize the risk of successful cyberattacks.

1. **Eliminating single points of failure:** One of the primary advantages of the Defense in Depth approach is that it prevents reliance on a single security product or measure. In a single-

layered security model, if an attacker bypasses the sole defensive mechanism, the entire system becomes compromised.

2. **Detecting and preventing a wide range of attacks:** By implementing multiple security controls at different levels, an organization can effectively detect and prevent a broad spectrum of cyber threats. Each layer of defense addresses specific types of attacks, such as network-based intrusions, malware infections, unauthorized access attempts, or data exfiltration.

3. **Limiting the impact of successful breaches:** if an attacker breaches one line of defense, the Defense in Depth strategy helps to contain and limit the impact of the incident. The additional security layers act as barriers that slow down the attacker's progress and provide opportunities for detection and response. For instance, if an attacker gains unauthorized access to a network through a compromised user account, they may still face challenges in accessing sensitive data due to encryption, access controls, or segmentation measures in place.

4. **Providing a holistic security approach:** Defense in Depth encourages organizations to take a holistic view of their security posture, considering all aspects of their IT infrastructure, including networks, endpoints, applications, and data. By implementing security controls at each layer, organizations can address potential vulnerabilities and risks comprehensively.

5. **Enabling rapid incident response and recovery:** Having multiple layers of defense in place also facilitates faster incident response and recovery processes. When a security incident occurs, the organization can quickly identify the affected layer and take targeted actions to contain and mitigate the threat. The presence of redundant security controls ensures that even if one layer is compromised, the other layers continue to provide protection, minimizing the overall impact of the incident.

Implementing Defense in Depth

Defense in Depth will require careful planning and coordination among teams, such as security, IT, network, and data owners, to identify the critical data, location, and classification level.

The company will need to do a risk assessment to identify risks that may affect the company's overall security posture. The organization must prioritize these risks based on their criticality. Finally, they must implement security controls or counter-measures to protect the data. They will also need to monitor the environment and update the defense continuously, as required.

Tips

Additional measures to add to their cybersecurity strategy to further bolster their Defense in Depth approach and minimize the potential impact of cyber threats.

1. Conduct periodic security audits and vulnerability assessments to identify and address any weak points in your current security infrastructure. This proactive approach can help you stay ahead of potential threats and ensure compliance with industry regulations.

2. Implement strong encryption protocols for sensitive data in transit and at rest. This adds an extra layer of protection, making it more difficult for unauthorized users to access and decipher sensitive information even if they gain access to your network.

Recap

This chapter introduced the concept of Defense in Depth, a comprehensive cybersecurity strategy that uses multiple security measures to safeguard an organization's information systems. The approach aims to establish a resilient security posture by employing diverse security mechanisms. Recognizing that no single security measure is entirely foolproof, this strategy combines various measures to mitigate the risks posed by different cyber threats.

Cyberattacks are an ever-present threat. Chapter 11 will equip you with the knowledge and skills needed to identify the signs of a cyberattack and implement effective response strategies to minimize damage, protect your assets, and maintain business continuity.

Chapter 11: Cyberattacks

Recognizing and Responding to Cyberattacks

Chapter 11 explores three essential topics. Firstly, we delve into malware detection and removal, addressing common malware and ransomware attack vectors, detection methods, removal techniques, and proactive security strategies for thwarting malware attacks. Next, we discuss Denial-of-Service (DoS) attacks, covering their definition, various types, detection methodologies, and mitigation measures companies can adopt to prevent DoS incidents.

Common Malware Attack Vectors

The Chinese general Sun Tzu said, "If you know the enemy and know yourself, you need not fear the result of a hundred battles." For a company to prevent malware and ransomware attacks, that organization must understand the tactics used by the attackers.

Phishing Emails: Malicious actors use phishing emails as a primary vehicle for disseminating malware, constituting the most prevalent delivery method. Upon interaction, such emails may contain attachments or hyperlinks designed to initiate the download and execution of malware and malicious code on the recipient's device. The prevention is user education on recognizing phishing email attempts and for the company to use email filtering and email security tools to help mitigate this vector.

Drive-by downloads: Malware can be automatically downloaded to a user's device when they visit a compromised or malicious website without user interaction. This attack leverages vulnerabilities in various Internet browsers, plugins, and apps. First, the malicious actor will find and exploit vulnerable websites, and then they will insert malicious code into the compromised website. When people visit these websites, the malicious code will scan their devices for vulnerabilities and exploit them. A way to prevent this is by regularly updating your browser, using web filtering tools, and employing endpoint protection to block malicious downloads.

Malicious Advertisements (Malvertisements): Malvertise-ments can appear on reputable websites and direct users to malware-infected sites or prompt unauthorized downloads. Prevention would include ad blockers, secure browsing habits, and keeping software updated to help prevent these attacks.

Infected External Devices: Malware can spread through infected USB devices, external hard drives, or other removable media devices. Prevention against this type of attack is to turn off Windows' Autorun features, scan external devices for malware, and educate users on the risk of using unknown external media.

Software Vulnerabilities: Threat actors will scan applications exposed to the Internet for known vulnerabilities to inject malware. This includes exploiting unpatched software or using zero-day vulnerabilities. That is why it is essential to update regularly and patch software, use vulnerability scanning tools, and employ intrusion detection and prevention systems.

Watering Hole Attacks: Attackers compromise websites frequented by the target audience, affecting these sites with malware. Users visiting these sites can unknowingly download malware. To prevent such risks, it is advisable to ensure that web browsers and plugins are regularly updated, employ web filtering tools, and exercise caution when accessing unfamiliar websites.

Malware Detection Methods

Malware detection and removal are critical aspects of cybersecurity to protect computer systems and networks from malicious software. There are various methods and tools employed to detect and remove malware. Here's an overview.

Anti-virus software can be very helpful, as it uses different techniques to find and block malware on your computer. One way is by checking files against a database of known malware signatures. If there is a match to one of the signatures known or saved, the anti-virus program will mark the file harmful and will not allow it to run.

Another technique is behavior monitoring, where the software watches how programs behave on your computer. It will block the program and alert you if it notices anything suspicious, like the program modifying important files. Some anti-virus programs also use heuristic analysis, which means they look for patterns of behavior that might indicate malware, even if they don't match a known signature.

Besides signature-based detection, anti-virus software may also use advanced techniques to detect and stop malware, such as anomaly detection, sandboxing, and machine learning.

Anomaly detection involves looking for unusual behavior or patterns that deviate from normal operations. If a program behaves strangely or accesses files, it shouldn't. The anti-virus software may flag it as malicious. Sandboxing creates a secure environment, known as a sandbox, where suspicious files or programs can be safely run and analyzed. This allows the anti-virus software to observe their behavior without risking harm to the rest of the system.

Machine learning involves training the anti-virus software to recognize malware based on patterns and characteristics found in large datasets of known malware samples. Over time, the software becomes better at identifying new and evolving threats by continuously learning from new data.

By combining these techniques, anti-virus software can provide comprehensive malware protection.

Malware Removal Methods

Discussing malware removal methods is essential if your system becomes infected with malware.

Automated Removal: An anti-malware tool will quarantine and remove the infected file, isolating it to prevent further harm to your system. Typically, quarantined files are encrypted and relocated to a secure location.

Manual Removal: Despite having antivirus or anti-malware software installed on your computer, manual removal may be necessary, particularly when dealing with sophisticated or new malware that lacks a known signature. Manual removal will involve identifying and deleting malicious files, terminating malicious processes, and cleaning up system configurations. As a word of caution, this should be done by a trained professional with in- depth knowledge of the malware and system architecture so you don't damage the system.

System Restoration: Sometimes, it might be easier to restore or revert the system to a previously clean state using backups. This method eliminates the malware but may cause data loss if recent changes are not backed up. After that, you must reinstall the software. Sometimes, the best solution is to uninstall and reinstall affected software to ensure a clean, malware-free environment.

Use Removal Tools: Security companies sometimes create tools to remove malware. These tools target and eliminate particular types of malware. Microsoft has Windows Malicious Software Removal Tool (MSRT) for Windows. This tool will find and remove specific, prevalent threats and reverse the changes they have made to your system. In the next section, we will talk about some best practices that you can use to prevent malware infections.

Malware Prevention Best Practices

A company can adopt several effective strategies to mitigate the risk of malware infection.

Regular Software Updates and Patching: The company needs to establish a robust vulnerability management and patching program, ensuring that operating systems, software, and applications are promptly updated to address potential vulnerabilities exploited by malware.

User Education: This involves periodic monthly or quarterly training sessions to educate users about the dangers posed by phishing emails, downloading files from unfamiliar sources, and visiting dubious websites.

Network Security: Network security is vital for an organ-ization to secure its computer network and data. As such, it is important to ensure that firewalls, intrusion detection systems, and intrusion prevention systems are configured and operational to monitor and control network traffic.

Continuous Monitoring: A company needs to have a holistic view of what is happening across its entire environment and be alerted quickly. It needs to employ a security information and event management system (SIEM) to continuously monitor and analyze system logs for signs of abnormal activity.

Use the EDR Solution: EDR stands for Endpoint Detection and Response. It is a cybersecurity solution that provides advanced threat detection, investigation, and response capabilities at the endpoint level. EDR solutions often include automation capabilities for incident response. In such a scenario, compromised endpoints are automatically isolated, malicious processes are blocked, or predefined response actions are initiated to contain and mitigate the impact of a security event.

Incident Response Plan: The plan must be updated to ensure a swift and effective response to a malware incident. Organ-izations and individuals can significantly benefit from adopting a multi-layered approach that combines these detection and removal methods with proactive security measures, dramatically enhancing resiliency against malware threats.

Ransomware Recovery Options

Addressing a ransomware attack presents significant challenges; however, various recovery options exist. Companies can proactively safeguard themselves and initiate recovery processes following such attacks.

1. **Isolation and Containment:** The organization must imme-diately isolate the affected systems to prevent the ransomware from spreading further. They can disconnect compromised devices from the network to contain the impact without turning them down, as doing so will remove critical evidence for analysis and investigation. Containment will limit the scope of the attack and provide them with time to evaluate the situation.

2. **Restore from Backup:** In the event of a ransomware attack, organizations can use their backups to restore data. Doing so will help the organization recover its data without paying the ransom and minimize downtime.

3. **Incident Response Plan:** The organization will need to closely follow their incident response plan. Following a predefined plan will ensure a structured response and reduce the attack's impact.

4. **Use of Decryption Tools:** Security companies and law enforcement agencies sometimes release decryption tools for

specific ransomware variants. These tools can decrypt files without paying a ransom. However, they may not work for the latest ransomware attacks, but companies can still check with cybersecurity organizations for available decryption tools that match the specific ransomware strain. The <u>No More Ransom</u> project is an excellent place to start.

5. **Engage Law Enforcement:** It is necessary to report the ransomware attack to law enforcement agencies. While they may not help or provide direct solutions, their involvement can aid in investigations and the identification of threat actors. Law enforcement cooperation may lead to the apprehension of attackers and the release of decryption keys, but that will also satisfy legal and insurance requirements.

6. **Security Software and Updates:** An additional measure organizations can take is to verify that their security software is operational and regularly updated. If not, they need to address that issue first. Updated security software can prevent reinfection, and patched systems are less susceptible to future attacks.

7. **Negotiation and Payment Considerations:** As a last resort, they may need to negotiate. Some organizations may consider negotiating with the attackers or paying the ransom as a last resort. This option is highly discouraged because of the ethical and legal implications and the uncertainty of receiving a valid decryption key. The organization will need to consult its legal counsel before making that decision.

A comprehensive cybersecurity strategy involves a combination of preventive measures, proactive planning, and effective response options. Regular updates and patches are needed to mitigate the impact of malware and ransomware attacks.

Denial-of-Service (DoS) Attacks

In this section, we'll dive into one of the most established forms of cyber extortion: the denial-of-service attack. Our exploration will encompass the definition of a denial-of-service attack and an examination of the various types that exist. We'll address the concept of distributed-denial-of-service attacks. Finally, we'll discuss strategies for detecting and mitigating these attacks.

DoS Attacks and Common Types of DoS Attacks

In chapter three, we talked about the CIA Triad principles, and we explained that the principle of availability is to ensure the systems are available to authorized users when needed. However, a notable threat to this principle is the denial-of-service attack, which aims to disrupt or prevent access to systems and services. A Denial-of-Service attack is a malicious attack where a company's network or website is flooded with false requests to disrupt business operations. Such attacks fall into four major categories: TCP/IP attacks, volume-based attacks, protocol exploitations, and application layer attacks.

TCP/IP attacks: One type of TCP/IP attack is the SYN flood attack. In a SYN flood attack, the attackers will flood the target with high-volume data requests it can't handle, causing it to slow down or crash. The system is so overwhelmed that it can't respond to legitimate requests. An example would be getting a table at a busy restaurant. But picture someone filling up all the seats with fake reservations, making it impossible for you and others to get in and enjoy your meal. That's what a Denial- of-Service attack does to a computer system.

Volume-Based Attacks: In volume- based attacks, the attackers can perform what they call a ping flood, sending a large number of ping requests to a target, consuming its network bandwidth, and making it unresponsive to legitimate traffic. They may execute what is known as a UDP reflection attack, where the attacker will exploit vulnerable UDP services to amplify the volume of the attacks sent to the target, overwhelming its resources.

Protocol Exploitation: In this scenario, attackers can send echo or ping requests to broadcast addresses, causing multiple systems to respond to the victim and amplifying the attack. This is called a Smurf attack. Attackers may employ DNS amplification, leveraging a vulnerable DNS server to amplify the volume of traffic directed at the target.

Application Layer Attacks: In an application layer attack, the attackers will flood the web server with a high volume of HTTP requests, consuming the server resources and making the website unavailable.

DDoS Attacks

Distributed Denial of Service attacks are malicious attempts to disrupt the normal function of a targeted server, service, or network by overwhelming it with a flood of traffic. Unlike traditional denial-of-service attacks, distributed denial-of-service attacks involve multiple sources and are often coordinated and distributed globally, making them more challenging to mitigate. The primary goal of the Distributed Denial of Service attack is to make a service or a website unavailable to its intended users.

Detecting and Mitigating DoS Attacks

The earlier you can identify an attack in progress, the quicker you can contain the damage. Detection, real-time monitoring, and responsive systems represent the optimal defense mechanisms against denial-of-service attacks.

DDoS Detection and Prevention Methods

Here are some detection and prevention methods companies can use or implement to prevent denial-of-service attacks and distributed denial-of-service attacks.

1. **Traffic Anomaly Detection:** They should deploy a traffic anomaly detection system to monitor unusual traffic patterns, such as sudden spikes or unexpected fluctuations. Employing anomaly detection tools can effectively identify ongoing attacks. Initially, they must establish a baseline for typical organizational traffic. Subsequently, they can implement an anomaly detection algorithm to pinpoint deviations that could signify a potential denial-of-service attack.

2. **Signature-Based Detection:** The companies can employ intrusion detection and intrusion prevention systems that use signature-based detection to identify known patterns associated with denial-of-service or distributed denial-of-service attacks and to block them.

3. **Deep Packet Inspection (DPI):** Another option is to use Deep Packet Inspection (DPI) to analyze packet payloads and detect patterns or signatures associated with distributed denial of service attacks. It will enable them to respond quickly and withstand a large-scale attack.

Collaboration with ISPs: By working together, they can implement upstream traffic filtering and blocking measures. This proactive approach prevents malicious traffic from reaching the target network. By implementing a combination of these mitigating controls, organizations can significantly reduce the risk and impact of a distributed denial-of-service attack, ensuring the continued availability and performance of their systems and services.

Tips

Here are some tips that you can implement right away:

1. Purchase anti-malware software to protect against malware and drive-by downloads.

2. Practice security hygiene by keeping your Windows or Mac computer up to date. You should keep your browser and all other applications you use regularly updated to maintain robust security measures.

3. Ensure you back up your data to cloud storage options like Google Drive or an external hard drive. This practice allows you to restore your data from a clean copy if your computer gets infected with malware. Remember to back up your data regularly to ensure the information remains current and up-to-date.

Recap

This chapter covered three critical topics. In the first segment, we explored malware detection and removal, discussing various malware types, threat vectors, and strategies for safeguarding against malware attacks. Moving on to the second segment, we talked about ransomware attacks and mitigation strategy. We concluded with denial-of-service attacks, detailing their types and continuity and discussing detection and mitigation strategies.

In Chapter 12, we'll examine business continuity and incident response planning. We'll emphasize their significance as a strategic approach for organizations to manage cyber threats effectively.

Chapter 12:
Beyond the Unexpected:
Building Robust BCP and
Incident Response Strategies

We'll examine the critical aspects of planning for and responding to unforeseen events that can disrupt business operations. This chapter underscores the importance of business continuity planning (BCP) and incident response (IR) strategies in safeguarding organizational resilience and ensuring minimal downtime during disruptions. We'll explore the fundamentals of creating robust BCP and IR plans, along with best practices, to enhance their effectiveness.

Business Continuity Planning

Business continuity planning (BCP) is a vital component of an organization's overall risk management and cybersecurity strategy. In today's digital landscape, where cyber threats are becoming increasingly sophisticated and prevalent, having a well-defined BCP is essential to ensuring that businesses can maintain their critical operations and services in the face of potential disruptions caused by cyberattacks.

BCP is a comprehensive tactical process that involves identifying, assessing, and planning for various risks and disruptions that could impact an organization's ability to function effectively. The primary goal of BCP is to safeguard an organization's critical functions, minimize downtime, and facilitate a swift recovery during unforeseen incidents, such as natural disasters, cyberattacks, power outages, or other emergencies.

Key Features of a Business Continuity Plan (BCP)

A Business Continuity Plan (BCP) is a comprehensive strategy designed to ensure an organization's critical functions can continue or resume swiftly in the face of unexpected disruptions, encompassing key features such as risk assessment, continuity strategies, and recovery protocols.

Business Impact Analysis: The first step in creating a BCP involves identifying the organization's most crucial functions and processes. This process is also called business impact analysis. It could include IT systems, communication channels, key personnel, etc.

Perform a Risk Assessment: The BCP process will consider potential risks and threats that could disrupt these critical functions. Among these are natural disasters, power outages, interruptions in supply chains, and, most importantly, cyberattacks. Understanding these risks will help the organization develop targeted contingency plans.

Create The Contingency Plans: The BCP process will create detailed contingency plans once the risks have been identified. For each critical function of the organization, there should be a plan that outlines how to maintain and restore it in the event of a disruption. This includes backup strategies, alternative resources, and communication plans.

Data Backup and Recovery: The BCP ensures data is regularly backed up and can be quickly recovered. This is crucial in cyberattacks, where data loss or system downtime can have severe consequences.

Employee Training: The employees must understand their roles and responsibilities for the company to recover successfully. It ensures everyone is on the same page and can contribute effectively to the organization's recovery.

Infrastructure Resilience: The BCP plan will have measures to enhance the strength of the critical infrastructure, including IT systems. It entails redundant systems' failover capabilities and infrastructure that can withstand cyber- attacks or other disruptions.

Regular Testing and Updates: When it comes to BCP (Business Continuity Planning), it is not a onetime effort; what is in fact important is the ongoing process, the refinement of which is a continuous process. The organizations need to regularly rehearse their plans by using various scenarios, exercises, and training in order to figure out weak points and mark progress. The training may be conducted as a tabletop exercise whereby the business leaders discuss scenarios as if they were already happening and the responses required, or as full live drills that simulate incident intervention by the business operations. Through the tests, organizations can evaluate the efficiency of their plans, see other programs' defects, and find means of perfection, which are important steps to getting more resilient.

Along with that, BCP must be updated frequently as technology advances, the number of staff increases, or the business environment changes. With new technologies, staff changes, and the business environment often altering, organizations must ensure their BCP remains relevant and useful if they hope to operate successfully. Achievement of this entails a constant check, assessment, and change of the plan and its various components in order to cope with the impedance caused by the shifting security landscape.

Communication Plan: Effective communication during a crisis is the key to keeping your internal and external stakeholders informed, which can help to maintain transparency and manage your reputation by taking care of your organizational image. Effective communication plans would consist of not only tactics for getting information out to employees, customers, partners, and key stakeholders but also the steps to be followed in receiving and responding to media inquiries and social media requests.

Incident Response and Reporting

This segment will examine Incident Response and the essential components of an Incident Response plan. Incident Response entails proficiently handling cybersecurity incidents, pinpointing their underlying causes, and executing strategies to avert future incidents.

Incident Response Plan

The Incident Response Plan (IRP) is a structured way of systematizing the actions that will be undertaken by the organization in the event of a cybersecurity incident or any other event of the kind that may threaten the confidentiality, integrity, or availability of the information systems. The primary goal of an IRP is to efficiently and effectively manage and mitigate the impact of incidents, minimize downtime, and restore normal operations as quickly as possible. An incident response plan document must be created with people's clear roles and responsibilities, steps for incident identification and classification, containing and remediating the incidents, and information distribution and reporting regulations.

Through a solid IRP, organizations can dramatically decrease the level of business losses resulting from cybersecurity incidents, ensure business continuity, and, of course, protect the company's reputation. Next, we are going to explore some major components and characteristics of an incident response plan to get an idea of how organizations withstand cybersecurity incidents.

Key Features of an Incident Response Plan

The initial component of an IRP is incident definition and categorization. It's crucial for the company to precisely outline what qualifies as an incident within its operational framework and then classify incidents according to their severity and potential operational impact. Responding to incidents can incur significant costs in terms of time, resources, and finances. Hence, proper classification of incidents is imperative for efficient management. Some of the most common security incident types include phishing and social engineering attacks, Distributed Denial of Service attacks, supply chain attacks, and ransomware. The IRP should cover these other components:

1. **Build a Team:** The organization needs to identify and designate members of the incident response team and their respective roles. These roles may include incident coordinators, investigators, communicators, and technical specialists. This will ensure everyone understands their duties during an incident.

2. **Have a Communication Plan:** During an incident, it will be necessary to communicate with different stakeholders and outside parties. A good communication plan will define how internal and external communication will be managed during an incident, the communication channels, the stakeholders, and the notification procedures to follow.

3. **Escalation Procedures:** Not all incidents require upper management involvement, so a good incident response plan will establish criteria for escalating incidents to higher levels of management or involving external entities such as law enforcement and regulatory bodies.

4. **Legal and Regulatory Compliance:** Based on the industry the company is in, you may have specific regulatory requirements. The incident response plan should align with legal and regulatory requirements applicable to the organization's industry, data breach notification laws, and reporting obligations.

5. **Preparation and Training:** We like to call it *practice how you play*. The organization must conduct regular Tabletop exercises, simulations, and drills to ensure the incident response team is

well-prepared to handle different incidents and identify areas requiring improvement. Update the plan based on lessons learned from the exercises.

6. **Incident Detection and Reporting:** You must define procedures for detecting incidents and require employees to report them promptly. It can be via email or a dedicated line to the security team.

7. **Incident Analysis and Assessment:** Once an incident has been reported, you need a process for quickly analyzing and assessing its nature, its impact on systems, data operation, and the scope of the incident.

8. **Containment and Eradication:** The company must outline procedures for containing the incident to prevent further damage and eradicate the root cause. This may involve isolating affected systems, removing malware or closing vulnerabilities, and defining protocols for preserving evidence related to the incident. Evidence preservation is crucial for forensic analysis, potential legal actions, and understanding the extent of the compromise.

9. **Recovery and Restoration:** Specify steps for recovering affected systems and restoring normal operations. Restoring data from backups, applying patches, and implementing additional security measures may be necessary.

10. **Post-Incident Review and Analysis:** Conduct a post-incident review to analyze the organization's response to the incident and identify areas for improvement in processes, technologies, or training.

11. **Continuous Improvement:** Use insights from incident response activities to regularly update and enhance the plan by incorporating the feedback loop into the IRP.

12. **Coordination with External Entities:** Depending on the incident, an organization may need outside help, so determine the circumstances under which external involvement is necessary and how you will coordinate with external entities, such as law enforcement, incident response organizations, and regulatory bodies.

13. **Documentation and Reporting:** Good documentation is valuable for audits, compliance, and future incident response efforts maintained through documentation of incident response activities, including timelines, actions taken, and lessons learned.

14. **Public Relations and Reputation Management**: If applicable, include plans for managing public relations and the organization's reputation during and after an incident. Define how and when to communicate with customers, partners, and the public.

15. **Integration with Other Plans:** The incident response plan is not a stand-alone plan. It must be integrated with other organizational plans, such as business continuity and dis-aster recovery plans, to ensure consistency and alignment across all response efforts.

By incorporating these key features into an incident response plan, organizations can effectively enhance their readiness to respond to and recover from a cybersecurity incident. The plan is crucial in minimizing the impact of incidents and maintaining the organization's overall cybersecurity resilience.

Tips

Practical tips that you can implement right away.

1. A Business Continuity Plan (BCP) is a comprehensive strategy designed to ensure an organization's critical functions can continue or resume swiftly in the face of unexpected disruptions,

encompassing key features such as risk assessment, continuity strategies, and recovery protocols.

2. Conduct regular training sessions for employees to familiarize them with BCP and IR protocols. This ensures everyone knows their roles and responsibilities during a crisis.

3. Regularly test your BCP and IR plans through simulated exercises or drills. This helps identify gaps, weaknesses, and areas for improvement in your strategies, allowing you to refine them for better effectiveness during actual incidents.

Recap

This chapter highlighted the indispensable role of Business Continuity Planning (BCP) in ensuring businesses can maintain essential functions during and after a disruption. We also emphasized the significance of Incident Response (IR) plans in effectively addressing and mitigating the impact of unforeseen incidents. Through understanding the key components and best practices of BCP and IR, organizations can better prepare themselves to navigate through crises and maintain operational continuity.

In Chapter 13, we will explore the exciting world of cybersecurity careers and the importance of continuous learning in this ever-evolving field. We will discuss various career paths, essential skills, and certifications, as well as strategies for staying updated with the latest trends and technologies in cybersecurity.

Chapter 13:
Cybersecurity Careers and Further Learning

Our last chapter will cover four key topics. First, we'll discuss the reasons for pursuing a career in cybersecurity and explore the various career paths available. Following that, we'll cover some of the cybersecurity domains. Next, we'll provide guidance on how to initiate your journey into cybersecurity and strategies for securing a job quickly. Finally, we'll explore the diverse learning opportunities essential for embarking on a career in cybersecurity.

Why Choose a Career in Cybersecurity?

Cybersecurity professionals are crucial in protecting organizations, individuals, and critical infrastructure from cyber threats. The increasing reliance on technology and the rise in cyberattacks create a high demand for skilled cybersecurity experts. By 2030, the growth market for cybersecurity professionals will go up by 33%, according to a report from the US Bureau of Labor Statistics. The following section will give ten compelling reasons to choose a cybersecurity career.

Ten Compelling Reasons to Choose a Career in Cybersecurity

1. **High Demand for Cybersecurity Professionals:** We are living in an increasingly digitized world. The frequency and sophistication of cyber threats have surged. As a result, organizations across industries are actively seeking skilled cybersecurity professionals

to safeguard their digital assets. The demand for cybersecurity experts far exceeds the talent, creating numerous jobs, opportunities, and career advancement prospects.

2. **Diverse Career Paths:** Cybersecurity offers various specializations, allowing individuals to tailor their career paths to match their interests and skills. Specializations include ethical hacking or penetration testing, incident response, security analysis, and more. This diversity enables professionals to continually learn and explore different facets of cybersecurity throughout their careers.

3. **Global Significance:** cybersecurity is a global concern, and professionals in this field contribute to protecting critical infrastructure, sensitive data, and national security. The work done in cybersecurity has a direct impact on global digital stability.

4. **Constant Evolution and Innovation:** Cyber threats are dynamic, evolving entities, and cybersecurity professionals are constantly challenged to stay ahead of the criminals. As a result, continuous learning and adaptation to new technologies, tools, and techniques are required to foster a dynamic and intellectually stimulating work environment.

5. **Competitive Salaries:** The high demand for cybersecurity skills has led to competitive salaries for professionals in this field. As organizations recognize the importance of cybersecurity, they will invest significantly in hiring and retaining skilled individuals.

6. **Job Security:** Cybersecurity professionals enjoy high job security due to the persistent and growing nature of cyber threats. The need for cybersecurity experts will continue as long as digital systems exist.

7. **Ethical Responsibility:** Cybersecurity professionals are crucial in protecting individuals, organizations, and society from

malicious actors. Many individuals find great satisfaction in knowing that their work contributes to the greater good and helps maintain the integrity of digital systems.

8. **Continuous Learning Opportunities:** The fast-paced nature of cybersecurity requires professionals to stay informed about the latest technologies, vulnerabilities, and threat vectors. This constant learning keeps the job exciting and allows individuals to deepen their expertise.

9. **Networking Opportunities:** The cybersecurity community is known for its collaborative and supportive nature. Professionals often engage in knowledge-sharing activities, attend conferences, and participate in forums, creating valuable networking opportunities.

10. **Career Advancement:** Cybersecurity professionals can advance into leadership roles, such as the Chief Information Security Officer (CISO) or a security consultant. This field offers a clear path for career progression and development.

A career in cybersecurity provides a unique blend of challenges, opportunities, and the satisfaction of contributing to a safer digital environment. The field's rapid growth and global significance make it an attractive choice for individuals passionate about technology.

Cybersecurity Domains

Understanding cybersecurity domains is essential for newcomers, as it provides foundational knowledge and a holistic approach to the diverse areas of cybersecurity. This knowledge enables individuals to explore various career paths, identify security risks, and develop strategies for risk mitigation. Familiarity with the different domains facilitates effective communication with colleagues and stakeholders, ensuring clear and comprehensive discussions about security measures and requirements.

Recognizing the various domains encourages continuous learning and growth, as individuals are motivated to stay updated with the latest developments and advancements in cybersecurity. Knowing cybersecurity domains equips newcomers with the skills and insights needed to navigate the cybersecurity landscape effectively, foster professional growth, and contribute meaningfully to organizational security efforts. A cybersecurity domain is a focus area or environment where security controls must be applied to protect computer systems and networks against threats. While the specific domains can vary depending on the framework or model used, we are going to cover the most commonly recognized cybersecurity domains.

1. **Governance, Risk Management, and Compliance (GRC):** The GRC encompasses all the enterprise risk management (ERM) strategy, implementation, execution, and continuous monitoring of the security program to mitigate existing threats within an organization. It helps the organization develop a set of security policies, risk assessments, and regulatory compliance, keeping the company's security program and business models in line with relevant regulations and standards.

2. **Identity and Access Management** (IAM) focuses on managing and controlling user access to critical resources within an

organization's network, ensuring that only authorized users can access specific systems or data.

3. **Network security** focuses on protecting the integrity, confidentiality, and availability of data as it is transmitted across and within networks.

4. **Endpoint security** involves securing endpoints such as computers, mobile devices, and other connected devices from malicious activities and unauthorized access.

5. **Cloud security** addresses security concerns related to cloud computing environments, ensuring data protection, com-pliance, and secure access to cloud-based resources and services.

6. **Data Security:** Data Security aims to ensure the con-fidentiality, integrity, and availability of data throughout its lifecycle, from creation and storage to transmission and disposal.

7. **Application Security:** Concentrates on securing ap-plications, including web applications, mobile apps, and desktop applications, to prevent vulnerabilities that attackers could exploit.

We've only scratched the surface of cybersecurity domains. Therefore, aspiring cybersecurity professionals should thoroughly explore these areas to determine which best aligns with their personalities and skill sets. This exploration will increase their chances of succeeding in the cybersecurity field.

Cybersecurity Career Paths

The question often arises: Can I pursue a career in cybersecurity without a technical background? The answer is affirmative. Indeed, there are ample opportunities for individuals without technical expertise to excel in cybersecurity roles. As you gain experience in the field, you can explore avenues for acquiring technical skills through further education. In the realm of cybersecurity, both technical and non-technical roles play integral parts in safeguarding digital assets and mitigating cyber threats. Here's a short list of roles for both.

Technical Career Paths

Network Security Engineer: This role focuses on securing an organization's network infrastructure and implementing firewalls, intrusion detection, prevention systems, and VPNs. We have security analysts who will develop and implement security measures.

Penetration Tester (Ethical Hacker): we have penetration testers or ethical hackers. They conduct authorized simulated attacks on systems to identify vulnerabilities and weaknesses, helping organizations strengthen their security.

Incident Responder: Incident responders respond to and mitigate security incidents, such as cyberattacks or data breaches, to minimize damage and prevent further incidents. As your experience grows, you can transition into the role of a security consultant.

Security Consultant: Security consultants offer expert guidance on security measures, conduct risk assessments, and aid organizations in devising and executing robust security strategies.

Security Architect: The security architect involves designing and constructing secure systems and networks, considering both software and hardware elements to guarantee holistic security measures.

Cryptographer: Cryptographers focus on developing and implementing cryptographic systems to secure data and communication channels.

Malware Analyst: A malware analyst will analyze malicious software to understand its behavior, characteristics, prevention, and mitigation methods.

Security Researcher: Security researchers conduct research to identify and understand emerging threats and vulnerabilities, contributing to developing new security solutions.

Security Operations Center (SOC) Analyst: A SOC analyst will monitor and respond to security alerts, ensuring the continued security of an organization's systems.

Non-Technical Career Paths

Let's explore the non-technical career paths,

Security Policy and Compliance Analyst: A security policy and compliance analyst develops and enforces security policies, ensures regulatory compliance, and manages risk assessments.

Security Awareness Trainer: That person educates employees on security, best practices, policies, and procedures to reduce the risk of social engineering and human errors.

Security Project Manager: In this position, the individual manages and supervises cybersecurity projects, ensuring timely completion, adherence to budgetary constraints, and fulfilling security standards and requirements.

Digital Forensic Analyst: A digital forensic analyst investigates and analyzes digital evidence related to cybercrimes supporting legal proceedings.

Security Auditor: A security auditor assesses an organization's security measures, policies, and controls to ensure compliance with industry standards and regulations.

Policy Analyst (Cybersecurity Policy): That person focuses on developing and analyzing cybersecurity policies in alignment with organizational goals and industry standards.

Risk Analyst: A risk analyst assesses and mitigates cybersecurity risks, aiming to reduce potential threats and vulnerabilities.

Cybersecurity Trainer/Instructor: The cybersecurity trainer or instructor educates individuals on cybersecurity concepts, tools, and best practices within educational institutions or corporate environments.

Cybersecurity Attorneys specialize in cybersecurity laws. They help with contract drafting, data privacy, and risk assessment-related matters.

It is important to note that many cybersecurity roles may require a combination of technical and non-technical skills. As the field is dynamic, individuals often have the flexibility to move between technical and non-technical roles based on their interests and evolving skill sets.

Building a Career in Cybersecurity

Let's explore the realm of cybersecurity career development. To kick things off, we'll examine the importance of career path planning and how it can significantly impact your success in the field. We'll dive into various methods for gaining practical experience you can highlight on your resume. Specialization within a specific cybersecurity domain will also be discussed, along with the crucial role of networking and professional associations in expediting your job search process. We'll also cover effective networking strategies to bolster your career prospects.

Career Path Planning

One of the most common errors, particularly for newcomers to cybersecurity, is leaping into the field without a clear plan. Often, they invest significant time and money only to feel frustrated or, worse, realize that the field isn't for them. Career planning helps you clarify your goals and aspirations, identifying what you want to achieve professionally. It enables you to maximize your resources, including time, money, and energy, by having a clear roadmap to allocate them efficiently towards your objectives.

Planning for your career transition allows you to set realistic and achievable goals, breaking them down into smaller, more manageable steps to make the journey less overwhelming. It also helps align your career goals with your values, interests, and strengths, ensuring that your new career path is fulfilling and meaningful. To assist in this process, we've provided a downloadable list of cybersecurity domains at the end of this chapter. After researching these different fields, evaluating your strengths, interests, and unique abilities is beneficial to see how they align with your desired cybersecurity role. When assessing your readiness to transition into cybersecurity, it's vital to engage in a reflective process, asking a series of questions to pinpoint your strengths, areas for improvement, and the specific cybersecurity domains that resonate with your interests. Consider the following inquiries: For those with a technical background, ask yourself: Do I possess a solid understanding of networking principles, including protocols and network config-uration? Am I adept at navigating operating systems such as Linux, Windows, and Mac OS, along with their respective security functionalities? What programming languages am I proficient in, and to what extent can I utilize scripting languages like Python or Bash?

Consider these questions to assess your hands-on experience. Have I worked on cybersecurity-related projects or engaged in activities like penetration testing, vulnerability assessments, or setting up security controls? Do I have experience with cybersecurity tools and platforms commonly used in the industry?

Regarding your educational background, ask yourself: What is your educational background, and does it encompass any coursework or degrees pertinent to cybersecurity? Are you open to pursuing further education or certifications to augment your understanding of cybersecurity?

Consider the soft skills you possess that are pertinent to cybersecurity, such as problem-solving, critical thinking, and attention to detail. Do you actively stay updated on the latest industry trends and emerging threats? Are there particular areas within the realm of cybersecurity that captivate your interest? In terms of your learning ability, how swiftly do you grasp new technologies and adapt to shifts in the cybersecurity landscape?

For your career goal or aspiration: What are my short-term and long-term career goals in cybersecurity? How does transitioning into cybersecurity align with my overall professional aspiration?

By documenting your responses to these inquiries, you can gain insights into your current skill set and experience, enabling you to expedite your job search. You can also pinpoint areas for enhancement or skills you need to acquire, establishing a roadmap for your transition into cybersecurity. For instance, your roadmap might entail determining the steps you will take to bolster your expertise and understanding of cybersecurity. Will you pursue formal education, such as obtaining a cybersecurity degree, or seek mentorship from seasoned cybersecurity professionals?

Lastly, regularly evaluate your progress and refine your approach as needed. Remember, the cybersecurity field offers diverse opportunities. Aligning your skills and interests can aid in selecting a specialization that complements your background and preferences.

Practical Experience

Many aspiring cybersecurity professionals face a Catch-22 situation: they require job experience to secure a position, yet they need a job to gain that experience. The self-evaluation you have done previously should give you insight into existing skills or experience that you can leverage. To jog your memory further, consider the following questions.

Have you managed user access, including tasks like creating accounts, adjusting permissions, and revoking access? Such experiences can be framed as access control expertise.

Did you contribute to endpoint and data security efforts, such as database building and fortification? Perhaps you've handled tasks like installing antivirus software or resolving antivirus-related issues.

Have you supported or participated in preparing for audits like SOC2 or PCI? Have you been involved in drafting organizational policies and procedures? These instances constitute valuable GRC (Governance, Risk, and Compliance) experience.

Have you utilized application scanners to uncover vulnerabilities or conducted code reviews? These activities contribute to your application security knowledge.

While these questions are not exhaustive, they illustrate the experiences you can draw upon.

Now, suppose you lack direct experience in security or IT-related roles. How can you acquire practical experience to enhance your resume and increase your employability? There are numerous avenues you can explore to enhance your cybersecurity skills, and we will cover eight of them.

Firstly, consider joining a cybersecurity community where you can engage in discussions, share knowledge, and seek advice. Online platforms such as Reddit, Stack Exchange, and Discord channels provide valuable spaces for these interactions.

Another option is to look for local meet-up groups, conferences, and workshops that you can attend. If local options are limited, consider participating in virtual events. These events often include hands-on workshops and demonstrations where you can learn from experts and network with professionals in the field.

Consider enrolling in online courses that offer practical labs and hands-on exercises to deepen your understanding of cybersecurity concepts.

Look for internships and entry-level positions in cybersecurity. Practical experience gained in professional settings is highly valuable and provides insight into the day-to-day activities of cybersecurity professionals.

Develop a personal project portfolio to showcase your cybersecurity projects and expertise. Build a home lab environment to experiment with security tools and undertake projects such as writing vulnerability assessment reports or creating security policies. Participate in Capture the Flag (CTF) challenges and competitions offered by platforms like Hack the Box, Over the Wire, and CTF 365. These challenges provide realistic scenarios to hone your problem-solving skills and practical knowledge in a controlled setting. Network and seek mentorship from experienced professionals in the cybersecurity field. Building connections with industry veterans can offer opportunities to learn from their experiences and receive guidance on skill development.

Lastly, explore volunteering opportunities at local organizations such as churches or nonprofit groups like food banks. Offer to assist with IT or cybersecurity-related tasks to gain practical experience while giving back to the community. Remember, gaining practical experience takes time and dedication. Consistency is key. So, make a schedule for regular practice. Stay curious, and don't be afraid to tackle new challenges; practical hands-on experience is essential for skill development and enhancing your credibility in the cybersecurity community.

Specializing in a Cybersecurity Domain

Cybersecurity is a broad field, so knowing or doing everything is impossible. That is why you need to specialize in a specific domain, such as penetration testing, incident response, cloud security, or network security. The choice is yours. What are some reasons you want to specialize in a specific domain in cybersecurity besides the fact that it is a broad field? There are several advantages.

Specialization in cybersecurity offers numerous advantages that contribute to professional growth and success.

One significant benefit is the depth of expertise attained through specialization. By focusing on a specific cybersecurity domain, individuals can develop a profound understanding of the subject, becoming invaluable resources within their chosen field and earning the reputation of go-to experts.

Specialization enhances marketability in the job market. Employers actively seek specialists with in-depth skills and knowledge to address cybersecurity challenges, leading to increased career opportunities and demand.

Specializing facilitates easier skill maintenance. Staying current with the latest technologies, tools, and best practices is essential in cybersecurity. Focusing on a specific domain allows professionals to efficiently maintain their skills, ensuring relevance and staying up-to-date.

Specialization also streamlines the learning process, allowing individuals to focus on acquiring the specific knowledge and skills necessary to excel in their chosen field. This targeted approach results in a more manageable learning curve, reducing overwhelm and accelerating proficiency.

Developing expertise in a specific cybersecurity domain also boosts confidence. Specialized professionals feel more assured of their abilities, leading to improved performance and decision-making within their area of specialization.

Specialization often opens doors to leadership opportunities. Recognized as leaders in their field, specialists may take on leadership roles, such as team leaders, consultants, or subject matter experts, contributing to organizational decision-making processes.

Finally, specialization can expedite career advancement. As specialists gain recognition for their expertise, they are more likely to be considered for higher positions, leading to faster career progression and professional growth in leadership.

While there is value in having a broad understanding of cybersecurity concepts, the benefits of specialization, including increased expertise, marketability, and career opportunities, make it a strategic choice for many cybersecurity professionals.

Networking and Professional Association

Cybersecurity networking and professional associations are crucial to career opportunities and success. Firstly, networking provides valuable opportunities to connect with experienced professionals, allowing you to gain insights, advice, and guidance on navigating the complex landscape of cybersecurity careers. Engaging with established experts helps newcomers understand industry trends, emerging threats, best practices, and the specific skills in demand.

Secondly, active participation in professional associations fosters a sense of community and collaboration. Cybersecurity is a fast-evolving field, and being part of a network allows you to share knowledge, exchange ideas, and collaborate on solving challenges. This collaborative environment helps expand your skill set and gain diverse perspectives on cybersecurity. Networking is an effective avenue for discovering job opportunities. Many positions in cybersecurity are filled through referrals and recommendations. Building a solid professional network increases your chances of learning about job openings, accessing the hidden job market, and receiving referrals from trusted connections.

Professional associations also provide access to exclusive resources, events, and training opportunities. These resources can include workshops, webinars, conferences, and industry-specific publications. By participating in such activities, you can enhance your skill development. Stay informed about the latest tools and techniques, and position yourself as a proactive and engaging professional in the eyes of potential employers. Therefore, join networking groups such as meet-ups, the Information System Security Association (ISSA), Women in Cybersecurity, and the Cloud Security Alliance.

As you can see, networking and involvement in professional associations are essential components for anyone seeking a job in cybersecurity. Your connections within the industry will provide valuable insights, collaborative opportunities, and a bridge to get you a job quickly. Engaging with professional associations enhances your knowledge base, keeps skills current, and provides access to exclusive resources, ultimately contributing to a successful and fulfilling career in cyber-security.

Networking in cybersecurity is critical to getting you your first job and growing in the field. Unfortunately, many jobs in cybersecurity are not publicly advertised. Networking allows you to tap into the hidden job market by connecting with professionals who may know job openings or can provide referrals. Engaging with professionals lets you stay current on the latest trends, technologies, and challenges, giving you a competitive edge in interviews and discussions. You can also find a mentor who can advise, share experiences, and offer valuable feedback, helping you navigate challenges and make informed career decisions.

As part of your career strategy, it's crucial to establish a robust presence on LinkedIn by connecting with a minimum of 500 professionals in your industry. It may seem like a high number, but it significantly boosts your visibility on the platform. With more connections, your profile gains greater exposure through the LinkedIn algorithm, increasing the likelihood of recruiters and hiring managers discovering you first. Having an extensive network ensures that your achievements and contributions are seen by a broader audience, positioning you as an expert in your field. To enhance your networking efforts, create a list of target companies and seek employees in roles relevant to your career aspirations. Connect with them to expand your network and gain insight into potential opportunities.

Actively engage with your connections by interacting direct-ly or sharing content that resonates with your industry. This demonstrates your expertise and fosters meaningful connections. By consistently implementing this strategy, even as a newcomer, you can expedite your job search in cybersecurity and pave the way for career advancement.

Networking Strategy to Get You a Job Fast

A strategic networking approach is crucial for expediting your job search process. First, define your career goals in the cybersecurity field, identifying specific roles or areas of interest.

Next, optimize your online presence, particularly on LinkedIn, ensuring a professional online profile. Ensure you customize your connection requests when con-tacting other professionals on LinkedIn. Clearly express your intention and emphasize mutual benefits. You should target specific companies and industries that you want to work for. Attend online and in-person net-working events and career opportunities to connect with professionals, recruiters, and potential employers. Don't forget to engage in online communities and join forums to participate in discussions, actively show-casing your knowledge and commitment to the field.

You must follow up strategically after networking events or informational interviews, maintaining regular but respectful contact to stay on their radar. Create a networking schedule, dedicating specific weekly times to networking activities and treating it as an integral part of your job search route. Offer value to your network by sharing relevant resources, show-casing your knowledge, and fostering reciprocity. As we previously mentioned, consider joining professional as-sociations related to cybersecurity for additional net-working opportunities.

Seek mentorship within your network, identifying potential mentors who can provide guidance and share experiences. Be open to potential opportunities and remain open-minded about potential job roles, recognizing that temporary positions can lead to more permanent opportunities.

Continuing Education and Certifications

Because the cybersecurity landscape evolves rapidly, continuing education is essential to stay current. I encourage you to continuously learn through courses, workshops, and con-ferences and to pursue certifications relevant to your cybersecurity domain.

Learning Resources and Certification Paths

This last section of our book is going to be about the many paths open for someone who wants to kick off a career in cyber security. We aspire to guide you through the wide variety of choices and to provide information on the perks and dis-advantages that each of these systems possesses. If you are choosing a learning method, it is necessary to give thought to your individual preferences, career aspirations, and learning methods styles.

Cybersecurity Degree Programs

Embarking on a degree program can offer considerable advantages for those venturing into cybersecurity. Initially, such programs furnish students with a structured curriculum encompassing a wide array of cybersecurity facets, providing a comprehensive understanding of the field. They establish a robust foundation in disciplines like computer science and mathematics, which are invaluable adjuncts to cybersecurity proficiency.

Degree programs facilitate cultivating a professional network through interactions with professors and peers. This networking can prove instrumental in securing future opportunities and garnering insights from industry experts. Certain cybersecurity positions, particularly those in leadership capacities, may necessitate a degree for career progression, rendering a formal education imperative.

However, it's crucial to acknowledge the potential drawbacks associated with degree programs. Firstly, they entail a significant time and financial commitment, often spanning four years or more and involving substantial costs. Given the rapidly evolving nature of cybersecurity, there's also a risk of programs lagging behind industry advancements, necessitating supplementary efforts to stay abreast of emerging trends. Not all degree programs offer hands-on, practical experience, which is vital for translating theoretical knowledge into real- world skills. Despite these limitations, a well-structured degree program remains valuable for aspiring cybersecurity professionals, pro-viding a solid educational foundation and fostering invaluable networking opportunities.

Cybersecurity Certifications

Depending on where you are in your career, another option is to pursue cybersecurity certifications to secure employment or as a path to a promotion within an organization. Certifications provide cost-effective, flexible, and specialized training compared to the costly and lengthy degree program.

Possessing well-recognized certifications like CompTIA Security+, Certified Ethical Hacker (CEH), Certified Information Systems Security Professional (CISSP), and Certified Information Security Manager (CISM) can bolster your credibility. Employers often value such certi-fications as indicators of expertise. Such certifications can unlock job opportunities and pave the way for career advancement, particularly when complemented by practical experience.

However, certifications are not suitable for everyone. Some can be costly, with exam fees and study materials adding up over time. Additionally, many certifications require periodic renewal through continuing education, which can be time-intensive or by retaking the exam for a fee. While certifications validate theoretical knowledge, they may occasionally fall short in providing the hands-on practical experience that employers often seek.

Cybersecurity Boot Camps

Attending cybersecurity boot camps presents a quick avenue for diving into the realm of cybersecurity. These immersive pro-grams offer intensive learning experiences, emphasizing prac-tical and real-world skills acquisition. Tailored to provide rapid entry into the job market, boot camps serve as a viable option for career switchers and individuals seeking expedited skill enhancement. They facilitate valuable networking oppor-tunities, enabling participants to forge connections with in-dustry professionals.

Boot camps come with their own set of challenges. The rigorous nature of these programs demands full-time commitment over several days, necessitating a significant investment of time and energy. Although typically more affordable than traditional degree programs, boot camps still entail considerable costs. The quality of boot camps can vary widely, with some lacking the reputable credentials and comprehensive curriculum found in more established programs. Thus, while boot camps offer a fast- track route into cybersecurity, prospective participants should carefully weigh the associated time, financial, and quality considerations before enrolling.

Online Courses and Training Programs

Online courses and training programs provide cybersecurity courses catering to different skill levels, from beginners to advanced levels. Online courses offer flexibility, allowing learners to study at their own pace and schedule. They are often more affordable than degree programs or boot camps. With that being said, they are not for everyone. Some learners may struggle with self-discipline, motivation, or understanding the materials in such an environment. They need more interpersonal interactions and networking opportunities found in traditional settings. Finally, the quality of online courses can vary, and not all are created by recognized experts or insti-tutions.

Mentorships

Mentorships are valuable resources that assist individuals in mastering cybersecurity by offering personalized guidance and support. Unlike traditional training programs that are broadly focused, mentorship provides tailored advice that considers your preferences, strengths, and areas for improvement. Essentially, a mentor collaborates with you to customize lessons based on your unique goals and requirements.

Mentors are essential in imparting practical skills and on-the-job insights by sharing their own extensive experience in cybersecurity. This personalized guidance can help individuals navigate challenges, make informed career decisions, and acquire the expertise and hands-on knowledge needed to succeed in the field.

Mentoring not only offers guidance and advice, but also provides opportunities to expand your professional network. Mentors can introduce you to other professionals in your field, paving the way for potential collaborations, job opportunities, or expert insights. These connections can open doors to new opportunities, such as research partnerships or speaking engagements, enhancing your visibility within the cybersecurity community.

However, it's essential to recognize the challenges of finding a reliable mentor and sustaining a long-term mentoring relationship. An ideal mentor should possess expertise in your focus areas and be willing to invest time and effort in your growth. Their availability and level of engagement may vary because of their busy schedules, making it challenging to maintain consistent communication.

Similarly, the effectiveness of an educational program largely depends on the mentor's expertise and the real-time support they provide. While a mentor's knowledge may offer valuable insights into common challenges, it may not always encompass the latest advancements or technologies in the field.

Ensure that your mentor has a background aligned with your interests and possesses the knowledge and practical experience to guide you successfully. Mentorships should be effectively integrated with other personal development opportunities, such as courses, certifications, and hands-on experience.

Mentorships have to be properly integrated and combined with other training for personal development, like courses, certificates, and real hands-on experience.

Tips

Tips to Help You Succeed in Cybersecurity.

1. Evaluate your current skills, strengths, and interests to identify which cybersecurity career path aligns best with your abilities and passions. This will help you focus on your learning and certification efforts more effectively.

2. Engage with cybersecurity professionals through online forums, webinars, or local events. Building connections can provide insights into career paths, learning resources, and certification recommendations directly from industry experts.

3. Create a personalized learning plan based on the resources and certification paths discussed. Dedicate time regularly to study, practice hands-on skills, and stay updated with the latest trends and technologies in cybersecurity to remain competitive in the job market.

Recap

This chapter provided compelling reasons to consider a career in cybersecurity, exploring both technical and non-technical career trajectories. We covered effective strategies for trans-itioning into cybersecurity, aimed at optimizing success while minimizing time and financial investment. We explained how to get practical experience to bolster your resume. We under-scored the significance of specialization in cybersecurity and outlined a networking strategy conducive to expediting job attainment.

We concluded this chapter on learning resources based on your career goals, objectives, and learning style. Continuous learning is instrumental to staying relevant in this dynamic field, so we encourage you to keep learning.

Conclusion

As we wrap up this detailed exploration of cybersecurity, it's crucial to look back at the enlightening journey we've shared. We've navigated through the intricate landscape of cyber-security, delving into its core principles, dissecting various cyber threats and defense strategies, and recognizing the pivotal role of ethics and legal aspects in cultivating a secure digital environment.

Initially, we laid solid groundwork by understanding the significance of cybersecurity in our digital-centric world and the imperative to safeguard our digital assets. In the subsequent section, we progressed to identifying a range of cyber threats, from phishing scams to ransomware, along with defensive measures to counter these risks. We underscored the impor-tance of cybersecurity practices, like employing unique pass-words and adopting multifactor authentication, safe internet browsing habits, and protection against social engineering schemes to ensure our digital safety.

We explored the importance of securing home networks and mobile devices. We learned about the benefits of network segmentation in establishing a protected digital space for individuals and organizations alike. We delved into the array of cybersecurity tools and technologies organizations utilize to reinforce their digital infrastructure, such as firewalls and intrusion detection and prevention systems (IDS/IPS), which help to safeguard against cyber threats.

We also focused on strategies to detect, respond to, and mitigate cyberattacks, particularly focusing on denial-of-service (DoS) attacks. We shed light on the myriad of fulfilling career opportunities within cybersecurity, underscoring the value of continuous learning, professional growth, and networking to excel in this ever-evolving field.

I encourage you to harness the knowledge, skills, and insights gained throughout this journey. Whether you aspire to pursue a career in cybersecurity, enhance your existing knowledge, or simply stay informed and protected in today's digital age, remember that cybersecurity is a continuous learning process.

List of free Cybersecurity Tools to gain experience.

https://www.mycyberblueprint.com/this-checklist-reveals- how-to-become-a-guru-in-cybersecurity-using-tool-cheatsheet

https://bit.ly/3HtYpxx

About the Author

André is an unstoppable force in the cyber-security world! With over two decades of experience in IT and cybersecurity, he boasts a plethora of industry certifications and holds a master's degree in cybersecurity and information assurance. Throughout his disting-uished career, André has made significant contri-butions across diverse industries, including banking, automotive, healthcare, tele-communications, and manufacturing. His multifaceted expertise has earned him recognition as a distinguished guest speaker at internal conferences hosted by the esteemed American Association of Motor Vehicles, where he shares invaluable insights on cybersecurity topics.

André's passion extends beyond his professional endeavors. His commitment to safeguarding companies and consumers from data breaches is a personal mission to create a safer digital environment for all. He ardently believes that adhering to fundamental security guidelines should be second nature in our interconnected world. Fueled by this noble purpose, André is now channeling his vast knowledge and experience into an upcoming book poised to revolutionize the field. More than just a cybersecurity manual, this book serves as a beacon of hope for individuals aspiring to make a meaningful impact in their lives and in the cybersecurity sector. With a pronounced shortage of experts in the field, André aims to empower more individuals to step up and fortify our digital landscape.

Under André's mentorship, countless individuals have flourished into successful cybersecurity professionals. Through his online courses and hands-on platforms, he is committed to bridging the gap between technical and non-technical en-thusiasts, equipping them with the requisite experience and knowledge to seamlessly transition into cybersecurity. Outside the tech realm, André nurtures an insatiable thirst for knowl-edge, immersing himself in the latest cybersecurity advancements to stay ahead of the curve. When not safe-guarding cyberspace, he indulges in exploring diverse cultures and expanding his horizons. Amidst this blend of expertise and adventure, André finds solace in the harmonious tunes of jazz and classical music.

Ready to join André on this extraordinary journey and be part of a movement that secures our digital future? Connect with him on his website, www.cybermasteryacademy.com, or through his vibrant social media channels and Facebook group. In this online community, you'll gain exclusive access to André's expert tips, tricks, and insights on carving your path into the dynamic world of cybersecurity.

Together, let's forge a safer digital world and shape our futures in the rapidly evolving field of cybersecurity. Embark on this exhilarating adventure with André, where learning, exploration, and empowerment intertwine seamlessly!

This is a step-by-step guide into cybersecurity to help aspiring cybersecurity professionals get started.

https://www.mycyberblueprint.com/unlock-your- potentials-and-go-from-novice-to-cybersecurity-ninja-in-no-

time

https://bit.ly/47FU3OE